MAN'S PROBLEMS—
GOD'S ANSWERS

D0893155

MAN'S PROBLEMS— GOD'S ANSWERS

by

J. Dwight Pentecost

MOODY PRESS

CHICAGO

© 1971 by
THE MOODY BIBLE INSTITUTE
OF CHICAGO

Eleventh Printing, 1982

Library of Congress Catalog Card Number: 72-155685

ISBN: 0-8024-5178-0

Printed in the United States of America

Dedicated to
Gwen
with a father's love

CONTENTS

INTRODUCTION

We all live in an unredeemed body in the midst of an unredeemed creation, with an unredeemed nature within us. We have an enemy without who constantly oppresses us, and an enemy within that is ever present with us. We face innumerable problems in the physical, mental, emotional, and spiritual realms.

We are tempted to feel that the complexities of modern life cause the problems we face. But they have been with us from time immemorial. They are not new.

In the Word of God are the records of men who wrestled with just such problems, and in this volume we look into their experiences. In their defeats and victories is God's solution to our practical problems. A study of the Word convinces one that "whatsoever things were written afore-time were written for our learning" and that God has revealed His answer therein.

These studies were prepared, not as abstractions but with the needs of a congregation in mind, to enable God's people to find God's answer to the problems they face from day to day. May God grant that you who are beset by our adversary find God's help through a study of the lives of men He has brought to victory.

J. DWIGHT PENTECOST

1

God's Answer to

THE PROBLEM OF GUILT

HEBREWS 10:1-18

Guilt is one of the major problems that God's children face day by day. Even though we have been saved by the blood of Christ and all sins have been graciously forgiven, many are plagued by a remembrance of past sins and failures, of wasted life and squandered years. Consequently, they know little of God's peace as their daily portion. A stranger phoned me recently and asked: "Do you know anything about the Bible?" I said, "I've studied it some." She said, "I'd like to ask you a question. If a person has accepted Jesus as her Saviour and commits a sin, can she still go to heaven?" I replied, "Let the Bible answer your question," and quoted the Scriptures. She said, "Yes, but you don't know the sin I committed. If a person is guilty of such and such a sin, is it still possible for her to go to heaven?" It was my joy to point out that the blood of Jesus Christ, God's Son, cleanses us from all sin. The caller dissolved in tears and hung up the phone.

Shortly after returning from a ministry on the West Coast, I received a letter from California, which brought tears to my eyes. The writer was in her late 60s. As a young girl she had walked in paths of sin. Then as a young woman she came under conviction and went through an extended period of distress and turmoil. Seeking a knowledge of God and forgiveness of sin, she was told that Christ died for our sins;

11

and at that time she accepted Him as her personal Saviour. She wrote, "I heard you preach one night this past week. You indicated that you believed that a person who had accepted Christ could be certain that sins were forgiven and that the guilt of past sin was gone. I've lived the twenty-five years since I accepted Christ in constant fear and dread lest perchance what I did in my youth would exclude me finally from heaven." It was my joy to write to her and point to passages of Scripture to answer that the blood of Jesus Christ, God's Son, cleanses us from all sin.

A good part of my ministry outside of public teaching or preaching has been in the realm of counseling. The main problem for which people have come to me for help is that of guilt. They are not unbelievers but believers—people who have been saved and know that they have been saved, but whose lives are plagued by the past. For a long time I could not understand why so many were concerned about guilt. Then I realized that those to whom I had ministered formerly, were people born in at least nominal Christian homes, brought up in Sunday school and church, and whose lives had been molded to some extent by the Word of God. Many were not saved and knew only "churchianity" and not Christianity, but their lives had been guarded from gross sin because of that early exposure to the Bible and to the truth concerning Christ. But the majority of those to whom I am ministering now from week to week are individuals who came to know Christ when they were adults, who did not come from Christian backgrounds, whose lives were not molded by the truths of the Word and, consequently, lived in sin. Without the benefits of a knowledge of God's Word in their earlier life and their college and young adult years, they were involved in many things of which they are now ashamed. That life left an indelible mark upon them and they wrestle with problems of guilt.

The Word of God has an answer for this problem. Guilt is the individual's response to his consciousness of having violated God's holiness. Paul says in Romans 3:23, "All have sinned, and come short of the glory of God." That in which God glories above all else is His unchangeable holiness; His unalterable righteousness. God sets His own holiness as a standard, and anything that falls short of His holiness is classified as sin by Scripture. An individual who falls short of God's standard suffers the pangs of guilt. No man is so depraved that he does not have a conscience, and that conscience is the voice of God convicting him of his failure to attain God's standard of holiness and righteousness. No people on the face of the earth are so depraved that they are without this inner convicting voice that convinces them of their failure to attain the standards of God's holiness and righteousness. Therefore, man, apart from the work of Jesus Christ, is guilt-ridden, whether he is in a sophisticated city or in secluded jungles.

Paul testifies to the existence of this convicting work of God in Romans 2. He is showing that the Jews fall short of God's standard of holiness because they have violated the written law of God. The Mosaic law was given to Israel, with the requirements of divine holiness spelled out line upon line and precept upon precept. When Israel sinned they knew they were guilty because they had transgressed a known law and consequently were suffering the pangs of guilt. Then the question arises, Since the law was given to Israel, and the Gentiles did not receive a written law, are Gentiles guilty before God? Do Gentiles also suffer the pangs of guilt? Paul answers in the affirmative: Gentiles even without the law suffer fom guilt. He explains that "when the Gentiles, which have not the law [the law of Moses], do by nature the things contained in the law, these, having not the law, are a law unto themselves: which shew the work of the law [notice the next phrase] written in their hearts, their conscience also bearing witness, and their thoughts the mean while accusing or else excusing one another" (Ro 2:14-15). Man's conscience bears witness to the same thing that the written law of Moses bears witness to: the demands of divine holiness and righteousness. So Paul says that God has written the law in the heart of man so that the law, the conscience, convicts man when he falls short of God's holiness and becomes guilty before God. Any man who is guilty before God suffers the pangs of guilt.

When a man is guilty and suffering the pangs of guilt, he may try to cover his guilt in a number of ways. This is true not only of unbelievers but of believers also. Guilt is one of the greatest human drives. Sometimes it drives man in a mad pursuit of pleasure. He goes from round to round of pleasure-seeking to cover his guilt by that which he hopes will sooth or satisfy. He may seek to dull the pangs by using dope or alcohol to deaden his conscience and give him a false feeling of contentment or joy. But pleasure is only an attempt to cover the guilt of the conscience; it cannot give release from it. Another person may give himself in reckless abandon to a life of sin. This energizes the criminal who goes from one crime to another, seeking through some thrill in breaking the law to cover up the guilt of broken law within him. In another individual, guilt may take more socially acceptable forms of drive, so the man becomes totally immersed in his work or in some hobby to which he gives himself in constant restless activity. He works incessantly in order that he might work off some of the frustration produced by guilt. Or, in another, guilt may produce a restlessness so that the individual must be occupied continually with something—a magazine, the TV, a telephone conversation, or going constantly. Guilt drives a man to restless activity because when he is quiet, guilt raises an accusing finger and makes the man miserable.

A child of God may react to guilt in the same way as an unsaved man. Guilt may produce a feverish activity or a restlessness or a pursuit of pleasure that puts God out of the picture, that seeks to deaden the conviction of the Word of God, and the accusation of the Spirit of God who dwells within. The believer may manifest this restlessness in what seems to be perfectly good ways by going from one church service to another and by neglecting that which is his responsibility at home or at business; in so doing he is covering up guilt by frequent attendance at services, committee meetings, or Bible classes. Driven by guilt, he may seek to smother the accusing conscience with activities which he thinks God would approve.

In dealing with this problem of guilt, two different facets of the truth must be presented: the doctrinal and the practical. Since the practical must always be based on the doctrinal, we begin with the latter. In Hebrews 10 the apostle is writing concerning God's answer to guilt and a guilty conscience. He begins by saying that under the Old Testament sacrificial system there was no final solution to the problem of guilt.

> For the law having a shadow of good things to come, and not the very image of the things, can never with those sacrifices which they offered year by year continually make the comers thereunto perfect. For then would they not have ceased to be offered? because that the worshippers once purged should have no more conscience of sins (10:1-2).

This sacrificial system was not designed to give peace of conscience. Its purpose was to remind men that they were guilty. On the Day of Atonement the high priest took a goat and sacrificed it. Then the goat's blood was sprinkled on the mercy seat. God dwelt above the mercy seat in a cloud of glory, so that blood was put between the visible manifestation of God's presence and the broken law within the ark. So blood was put between God and the broken law. Then the priest took the second animal and, putting his hands on its head, confessed the sins of Israel over its head; then that scapegoat was led out into the wilderness to die. Sin was removed from the camp of Israel.

Did that last permanently? No, only for twelve months. As the believing Israelite started the new year, he could know that the blood was covering his sin and he had a feeling of peace. But as the year progressed, he became so miserable because of his guilt that he desired the Day of Atonement to come so the priest could put blood between a holy God and the broken law so his sin could be covered and removed. Every year Israel was forced by God to renew a note of indebtedness, for the blood of bulls and goats could not take away sins permanently. It could only postpone the time when payment was demanded, for it made only a temporary covering. Since Israel was covered by a temporary covering, God gave them a conscience concerning sin so that that note would be renewed year by year. If they had been once and for all purged, they would have had no more conscience about sin. "And having an high priest over the house of God; let us draw near with a true heart in full assurance of faith, having our hearts sprinkled from an evil conscience" (Heb 10:21-22).

An evil or guilty conscience no longer exists because there is cleansing, forgiveness, and restoration. Consequently there is no more need for an annual remembrance of sin. Guilt is gone. In verse 2 there was remembrance of guilt, and in verse 22 there is no more remembrance of guilt. Something has happened in between so that there is no more conscience about sin. What is it? Notice that the author says that Christ has made a voluntary sacrifice: "In burnt offerings and sacrifices for sin thou hast had no pleasure. Then said I, Lo, I come . . . to do thy will, O God. I come to do thy will, O God" (vv. 6-7, 9). Here Christ is contrasted with the Old Testament animal sacrifices. Animals' blood only had limited value. But when Christ came as the infinite Son of God to give Himself as a sacrifice for sin, His sacrifice was of infinite value.

Furthermore, every animal sacrificed in the Old Testament was an involuntary sacrifice which went to the altar of sacrifice against its will. A sheep or a goat can sense the presence of death or the smell of blood, and will instinctively turn and flee from the place where blood has been shed. The law said that the sacrifice had to be bound with cords to the horns of the altar because it was an involuntary sacrifice. That which was sacrificed against its will had little value in the sight of God. But when Jesus Christ came as the Lamb of God, He differed from all Old Testament sacrifices. He was a voluntary sacrifice. He said, "Not my will, but thine be done." That's the first thing that gives the guilty sinner a clear conscience.

Christ's sacrifice was a sufficient sacrifice. "This man, after he had offered one sacrifice for sin for ever, sat down on the right hand of God" (v. 12). Notice Christ's *one* sacrifice in contrast to the tens of thousands of sacrifices of the Old Testament. Even the blood of the goat on the Day of Atonement could avail for only twelve months. But Christ, whose blood availed forever, has given a sufficient sacrifice for sins.

Then the apostle points out that through this willing sacrifice we are sanctified through the offering of Christ's body once and for all (v. 10). We are *sanctified*—holy, or set apart. We were set apart by the sacrifice of Christ to God. We belong to Him because we became sons in His family. His name was put upon us. We are His.

Not only are we set apart but "by one offering he hath perfected for ever them that are sanctified" (v. 14). He hath *perfected*. God has to separate a sinner from Himself because He sees the sin in the sinner. But when the blood of Christ perfects us and removes every sin, there is nothing that God can find in us as a basis of condemnation. The glorious truth is that when we are covered with the blood of Christ, God looks upon us just as He looked upon His own beloved Son; and there is no more reason for God to reject the one who is covered by the blood of Christ than there is for God to reject Christ Himself. By His sacrifice we are perfected forever.

The Holy Ghost also is a witness to us (v. 15). It is the Spirit's ministry to assure us that we who have received Christ and believed in Him are the sons of God. John says, "He that believeth on the Son of God hath the witness in himself" (1 Jn 5:10). The Spirit bears witness with our spirit that we are the children of God. The Spirit says to the one ridden with guilt that Christ has voluntarily made a satisfactory sacrifice, that we have been set apart to God, and that we have been perfected so that in God's sight we are flawless. The Spirit convinces us of that truth.

The apostle concludes his argument in verse 17 by saying that the Father dismisses from His mind the memory of every sin that is covered by the blood of Christ. He is referring to Jeremiah 31:34, which gives the most glorious truth found in all the Bible, for God says, "I will forgive their iniquity, and I will remember their sin no more." The apostle was so impressed with this himself and wanted to impress it upon his hearers that he referred to it in Hebrews 8:12, "I will be merciful to their unrighteousness, and their sins and their iniquities will I remember no more." In dealing with the question about a guilty conscience, he affirms again, "Their sins and iniquities will I remember no more" (Heb 10:17).

Thus, the doctrinal argument of the apostle in Hebrews 10 shows how one passes from a guilt about sin to a guiltlessness about sin. That guiltlessness or clear conscience is the result of appropriating by faith Christ's work on the sinner's behalf. Freedom from guilt is not the result of sinless perfection; it depends on the value of Christ's blood which cleanses us from all sin.

Do you have that doctrine straight? Do you know that all your sins are under the blood of Christ? Do you believe the testimony of the Word that your sin has been dismissed from God's memory, and it is treated as though it had never been committed? Unfortunately we don't have the gift of dismissing from our minds that which brings guilt to our conscience. We've not been given that power, but God by a sovereign act of His will can and does dismiss from His mind the memory of every sin that has been covered with the blood of Christ. That is the doctrinal basis of a good conscience.

Then there is the practical side. How are we to respond to this doctrine? Peter says, "Be sober, be vigilant; because your adversary the devil, as a roaring lion, walketh about, seeking whom he may devour: whom resist stedfast in the faith" (1 Pet 5:8-9). Satan is called by the apostle John "the accuser of our brethren," (Rev 12:10). When a child of God commits a sin, Satan can take the occasion to appear in God's presence and accuse that believer before God (1 Jn 2:1-2). One of the adversary's tactics—since he cannot take away our salvation—is to take away the joy of our salvation. Since our sonship is settled, he seeks to keep us from enjoying it. One of his subtle methods of doing this is to remind us of some past sin. It may be something we did years ago which he delights to use to torment us. It may be something of which we were guilty before we ever came to know Jesus Christ as our Saviour. If so, when we accepted Jesus Christ as our personal Saviour, it was put under the blood; God has forgotten it but Satan hasn't forgotten. If God has dismissed from His memory every sin covered by the blood of Christ, then obviously that feeling of guilt cannot come from Him. The only other one who can cause it is Satan. Not only does Satan accuse us before God, but he accuses us before our own conscience. Thus the conscience that has been cleansed from sin's defilement is now aroused to consciousness over sins that are already dismissed in the mind of God; and the child of God breaks emotionally, mentally, or physically because he keeps on listening to Satan's accusations stirring up a conscience about guilt.

How are we to meet this? Peter says, "Whom resist stedfast in the faith" (1 Pe 5:9). To "resist" means to withstand. It is the same word Paul used in writing to the Ephesians concerning the armor of God: "That ye may be able to *withstand* in the evil day, and having done all, to stand" (6:13). The apostle says that when Satan accuses us, we have the right and the authority as the sons of God to forbid him to keep on accusing us because we believe what the Bible says that our sins are under the blood and are dismissed; there is no remembrance of them in heaven. How far can Satan get when he accuses the brethren before God? He doesn't get anywhere because we have an Advocate with the Father, Jesus Christ the righteousness, who pleads His blood. And Christ offers His blood to the Father as that which keeps on cleansing us from all sin. Satan can't get anywhere with God because Christ pleads His blood. What is our defense when Satan accuses us? The blood of Christ. We can silence the accuser of the brethren when he accuses our conscience and stirs up guilt over forgiven sins by pleading the efficacy of the blood of Christ. Peter commands us to resist him *"stedfast in the faith."* We believe that these sins are covered, and that there are no sins remembered by God; and if God

has forgotten them, what right has Satan to make us miserable about them?

John also says, "If our heart condemn us . . ." (1 Jn 3:20*a*).
This is the very problem about which we are talking: children of God who have some guilt about something in the
past. Our heart condemns us. What is the answer? ". . .
God is greater than our heart, and knoweth all things" (v.
20*b*). What does John mean? God knows that the blood of
Christ has already been applied to that thing and that the
blood of His Son, keeps on cleansing us from all sins (1 Jn
1:7). Peter said the same thing: "Resist [him] stedfast in
the faith"—that is, believing what God said. You don't have
to exhort God to believe what He knows is already true, because God knows that those sins are under the blood. If our
heart condemns us, we have this joy, that God is greater than
our hearts and knows all things. He knows that those sins
are under the blood.

But this disquieting fact often comes up: "Suppose I've
done something and I'm not conscious of it? Suppose I have
grieved the Spirit and maybe don't know about it?" Some
people are living in morbid introspection, always afraid that
they have done something and feeling miserable because
they can't pinpoint what it is. That's the problem John is
meeting when he says, "If our heart condemn us not, then
. . ." (1 Jn 3:21). Don't get worried about it. We have
"confidence toward God." Why? Because it is the ministry
of God the Holy Spirit to convict us of anything that dis-
pleases Him, and He'll do His work perfectly. Isn't it strange?
Some people get upset if they have guilt feelings and others
get upset if they don't have them. One is as wrong as the
other. The answer to both is the same. Trust God to do His
work. Jesus Christ will keep on applying the benefits of His
death to the believer so that he is always acceptable to God

the Father. And God the Holy Spirit will do His work of
convicting, reproving, rebuking, exhorting, to deal with anything in the present experience that may grieve the heart of
God. If we are guilty, then we must trust God. If we are not
guilty, then we still must trust the Spirit to do the work
which He has come to do.

Much has been written about this problem of guilt. For
the child of God it is relatively simple. There is danger in
oversimplification, but it is this simple: the child of God first
of all must know and accept the facts of the doctrine that
God has dismissed from His mind because of Christ's work
every sin of the person who has accepted Jesus Christ as
Saviour. That is a fact to be believed; it is the basis of our
assurance. If guilt arises, it does not originate from God. It
comes from Satan who is seeking to destroy our joy, and
Satan is to be resisted or rebuked (with the blood of Christ)
and the blood of Christ will silence this accuser of the
brethren. Don't listen to him. Don't entertain the suggestions and doubts he puts in your mind. Instead, claim the
efficacy of the blood of Christ and stand on the promise that
His blood cleanses from all sin. Praise God for the blessed
truth that God has affirmed that "their sins and iniquities
will I remember no more." The best way to deal with Satan
when he comes to make you miserable is to say bluntly, "Shut
up! My sins are under the blood." If that satisfies God, it
certainly ought to satisfy any one of God's children.

But there can be no easing of a guilty conscience until a
person comes to know Jesus Christ as his personal Saviour.
The truth presented here from the Word is for the benefit of
God's children who may be wrestling with this problem. But
it will not relieve your guilt one bit if you have never
accepted Jesus Christ as Saviour. You will continue to be
the most miserable person in the world until you have faced
this question seriously. God loves you and Christ died to

save you, but you must bear your own guilt until Jesus Christ takes that guilt away by covering your sins with His blood. Accept Christ personally as your Saviour now.

2

God's Answer to

THE PROBLEM OF SUFFERING

2 CORINTHIANS 12:1-10

Human experience substantiates the observation of Eliphaz when he said to Job, "Man is born unto trouble, as the sparks fly upward" (Job 5:7). It is a natural law, that is reversed only under the most unusual circumstances, that sparks from a fire ascend. Eliphaz in seeking to console Job reminded him of that fact.

Sorrow descended upon the human race because of the rebellion of Adam against God. Until Genesis 3, when Adam and Eve disobeyed and partook of the forbidden fruit, sorrow was a total stranger to the race. In judgment God placed on Eve the sorrow of childbirth and submission, and upon Adam, the sorrow of labor. All of Adam's descendants have been born to sorrow because of Adam's sin. And as we live from day to day, to varying degrees, we all experience the results of the fall. We live in an unredeemed body in the midst of an unredeemed creation with an unredeemed nature within us. We have been saved, we have been placed in Christ, we have been given an incomparable destiny; but as long as we walk through this life, we walk through that which we often refer to as the vale of tears.

Does the Word of God offer any help to those who are called upon to suffer? Three individuals from among the multitudes whose sufferings are recorded in the Bible are

24

examined in this chapter to see what they learned through their sufferings and to help us to learn from our sufferings.

A cardinal principle will deliver you from a great deal of anxiety and restlessness when you undergo suffering. When a trial or testing comes into the life of the average person, he instinctively asks, "What have I done to deserve this?" That infers that either God is dealing unjustly with men and that we don't deserve such testing, or that God is punishing us for some unknown sin, and we are seeking an explanation as to what it may be so that the suffering may be alleviated. It is true that God on many occasions deals in discipline with His child, but His Word makes it clear that the testings which God allows us to experience are not punishment in any sense of the word. Again, the suffering, the testing, and the trials through which we go are not punishment. Punishment is retribution for wrongdoing. It is a penalty inflicted for what one has done. If God were punishing us for what we did, we would experience nothing but trouble, trial and testing from morning to night. Jesus Christ in His death on the cross has borne the punishment for the guilt for our sin. Our sins were placed upon Him, and on the cross He paid the debt which we owe. That included sins that, as of this moment, are past, present and future. We recognize immediately that when Christ died, all of our sins were future, and they were gathered and placed on the Son of God who bore them in our place He was punished for us.

God would be unjust to exact a double payment. To punish Christ for our sins and then punish us for our sins would be exacting a double payment. When our sins have been covered by the blood of Christ, our debt has been paid; there is no need for God to exact a second payment by punishing us. If you as a child of God can grasp this cardinal fact that while God may discipline His child, He does not punish His child, it will give you an entirely different attitude toward your experiences. A child of God will rightly recoil from punishment by God, but he may joyfully embrace the discipline which God sends into the life, no matter how difficult it may be, because of the end in view.

God has become our Father through the Lord Jesus Christ. By the new birth we have been born into His family. He has a purpose for all His children, which is made clear in Romans 8:29. It is to conform us to the image of His Son. In accomplishing His purpose God knows just the instruments to use. He is a sculptor and He is trying to sculpt you into the image of Christ. If you were to put a block of marble in front of me and ask me to produce a replica of Michaelangelo's "Moses", I would be completely frustrated because I would not have the faintest idea as to how to go about chiseling a figure. Or you might ask me to reproduce DaVinci's "Last Supper," and give me a palate, brushes, and oils; but I could not do it because that's ouside my ability. Or you might give me a piece of steel and ask me to make it into a fine watch. There are those who can do it, but I can't; and I wouldn't know how to begin.

Every artist and craftsman has to know his material, his tools, and his design principles. Then he proceeds with the materials according to set principles with certain tools to accomplish the desired end. And when God purposes out of this material to reproduce Jesus Christ, He has the material and the pattern, and will select the tools. The wood-carver would not use the same instruments that the stone-carver would use because one kind of chisel is needed to carve wood and another kind to carve stone. The man working in wood could never produce a figure with stone-carving tools nor could the stonecutter carve wood with his tools. The tool and the material must fit each other. God in infinite wisdom knows just what tools to use to form the material with which He is working into Christ's image.

God is working with people. Wouldn't He use the same instruments on all people since He's working with the same material? No. Some people are soft and pliable in the hand of God just like the potter's clay, while God has to liken others of us as the prophet likened us, to flint. We are stiff-necked and hardhearted, unyielding, and we resist the forming work of the fingers of God. God has to deal with each individual individually as a separate mass of material in order to conform that one to Jesus Christ.

The book of Job deals in greater detail with this problem of suffering than perhaps any other portion of the Word of God. Every time we think of suffering, we think of the suffering of Job. He was called upon to suffer the loss of all of his material possessions, the loss of all of his loved ones, the loss of his position in his community, the loss of his physical health. He suffered as few men have suffered, and the book revolves around the answers to the problem. Job's comforters had no solution. Approaching the problem rationally, traditionally, and experientially, they offer no solution. But notice Job's words as he testifies as to what he learned through his suffering: "Then Job answered the LORD, and said, I know that thou canst do every thing, and that no thought can be withholden from thee" (42:2). Job was a righteous man; chapter 1 attests to that fact. Job was a religious man. He was a practicing priest in his family and daily offered sacrifice for his sins and the sins of his sons. He was a man after God's own heart, one who knew God; and yet, through this suffering, Job learned something of God that he had never learned before. God revealed Himself in a new way to Job and made Himself known to him. Job says that through the sufferings through which he had passed, he had learned of the power of God. "I know that thou canst do every thing." What kind of a God did he have? Not only a holy God who must be satisfied through blood sacrifices. Not only a God of dominion and majesty who is to be worshiped. But He is a God of power and might, a God whose arm can move on behalf of the one whom God takes into suffering. Job learned this lesson of God's power in suffering that he had not learned in the sanctuary as a priest ministering before God.

Through his suffering he had come to a personal, intimate, experiential knowledge of God. "I have heard of thee by the hearing of the ear: but now mine eye seeth thee" (42:5). What was it that made God so real? What was it that took God out of the expanse of the heavens and made Him seem personally present with Job? It was the suffering through which God took him. Job had been a worshiper. He had been a ministering priest before God, but to him God was a God afar off. He was not personally present. He was not vitally interested in Job as a person. Job says, "Now that I have walked through this vale of tears with God, I have seen something of God's power, and I now know Him personally and intimately." It was the sufferings that taught Job of God's personal presence with him.

Job learned another thing: "Wherefore I abhor myself, and repent in dust and ashes" (42:6). In the sight of God, Job was nothing. He might have been the wisest man of his generation. He might have been the richest man. He might have been the most influential, powerful man politically in his generation. He had everything to make him proud and to be satisfied in the flesh. But when he saw God, he had to say of himself that he was nothing. There is nothing like the experience of suffering to reveal to a man exactly what he is. When God takes a man through testing, it is impossible for that man to consider himself self-sufficient any longer. Although Job found the sufferings very difficult, he also found them worthwhile. The God who was exalted and powerful became a personal reality in his experience, and he knew

that he had been sustained by the arm of God, that he could
lean back upon the shoulder of God, and that he could then
feel the heartbeat of the love of God. The suffering through
which he had passed had taught him these personal intimate
lessons. Job's knowledge was theoretical until God took
everything away and stripped him of all that he possessed.
Then he learned the sufficiency of God Himself. Job may
have been tempted to trust his wealth, his position, or his
friends; but when they were gone, what did he have left? He
found that he had God. When did he know that he had God?
Only when everything else was taken away, and Job through
his sufferings could say, "I have heard of thee by the hearing
of the ear: but now mine eye seeth thee" (42:5). So Job's
suffering brought him to a personal, intimate knowledge of
God and to dependence upon God for his strength.

Another classic example of one who was taken through
suffering is recorded in John 9. This man's suffering was not
of a relatively short duration as was Job's. He suffered over
an extended period of time, for he had been blind from
birth. This was viewed by the Jews as a divine judgment for,
according to Jewish theology, all suffering in the physical
realm was a result of sin. Either this man had committed a
sin in some former existence, these Pharisees reasoned, or
else his parents had sinned. God had said that He would
visit the iniquities of the fathers upon the children unto the
third and fourth generation; so when they saw this blind
man, they reasoned that somewhere in his lineage was some
sin that caused God to bring this divine visitation upon him.
The question was asked by the disciples: "Who did sin, this
man, or his parents, that he was born blind?" (Jn 9:2)
Christ's answer reveals another purpose for suffering: "Neither hath this man sinned, nor his parents: but that the works
of God should be made manifest in him" (9:3). This man
was born blind and lived his life in blindness so that when

the appointed day should come when the Son of God would pass by and would touch this man's eyes he should be made to see. He was prepared by God from the time of his birth so that he would be an instrument to reveal Christ's power and glory to his generation.

Christ came into the world and made the most startling claim that a man had ever made. He claimed to be the Son of God. If this was not true, it was the most blasphemous assumption that a man could possibly make. He claimed to be the Messiah, the Deliver of Israel. In so claiming, He was asserting an authority and a power greater than the Roman Empire, greater than Caesar. He called Himself the Son of God and a greater man than Caesar. He promised forgiveness of sins to those who would trust Him. Such claims needed to be authenticated. If Jesus Christ was what He claimed to be, He had to be able to demonstrate it. Because not everybody in Israel was hale and hardy, there was opportunity for Christ to demonstrate what He could do in the spiritual realm by what He did in the physical realm. He demonstrated that He could cure the walk of Israel as they stumbled along in sin by curing those who were physically lame. He proved to Israel that He could open ears that were deaf to the Word of God by healing those who could not hear physically. He proved that He was the light of the world and could give spiritual light to man by healing blind men. He proved that He was the resurrection and the life by raising those who were physically dead. Christ used men with physical infirmities to demonstrate His spiritual power. This man was born blind, not because of his sin or his parents' sin but that Jesus Christ should have one through whom He could demonstrate His power to that generation.

The world today is looking for proof of the power and the authority of Jesus Christ. Where does the world see it? It is seen as the Son of God touches this one, transforms that one, takes this one through some testing and in the testing gives him joy that doesn't come from within but that comes from above. As the worlding sees the child of God enduring the testing as from God with joy and in complete submission, then the world has evidence of the power and the authority of Jesus Christ. When this blind man stood whole before his generation, he could bear this testimony: "Since the world began was it not heard that any man opened the eyes of one that was born blind. If this man were not of God, he could do nothing" (9:32-33). This man was prepared by God as an instrument to show forth the power, the authority, and the deity of Jesus Christ. Many times God takes His children through testings in order that they may be instruments to bear witness to Christ's power and glory.

In 2 Corinthians 12, as on other occasions, the apostle Paul was called on to defend himself against certain false charges. The charges leveled against him were that he was an idle boaster, that he was seeking glory for himself. This arose out of the fact that Paul had received greater revelation in divine truth than had been given to any man up to this point in time. Paul was God's chosen instrument to reveal divine truth to man. God caught Paul up into glory and revealed things concerning God to him, some of which he was forbidden to speak, the rest of which he was to communicate through his epistles. As people heard the revelation from Paul, they may have supposed he would use his privileges to promote himself. But Paul said, "And lest I should be exalted above measure through the abundance of the revelations, there was given to me a thorn in the flesh," (v. 7). God recognized that no man is impervious to the temptation of pride, not even the apostle; and the one who could say of himself, "I am the least of all the apostles," was still temptable with pride. But to prevent any manifestation of pride, God gave Paul a thorn in the flesh. It was a messenger of

Satan to buffet him in order to keep him dependent upon God.

When Paul talked about the thorn in the flesh, it wasn't a little prick such as one gets from a rosebush. He wouldn't have talked about being buffeted had it been something insignificant. This was a very serious and grievous suffering. It extended over a period of time because he said he prayed to the Lord three times that this thorn might be taken away; but God chose to deny his request. Why was Paul taken through this suffering? He says that in the first place it was to prevent the sin of pride. When we pray about this matter of humility, we always pray, "Lord, keep me humble." What does that say? "I am as humble as I ought to be; now You just keep me that way." When was the last time you ever heard anyone pray, "Lord, make me humble"? There is a vast difference. Pride led Satan into his first sin against God. And in order to keep Paul, who was mightily used by God, from disgracing the name of Christ by being given over to pride, God sent the thorn to make him humble. And so he said, "Lest I should be exalted above measure . . . there was given to me a thorn in the flesh" (v. 7). Notice that he repeats again: "Lest I should be exalted above measure."

There is a second reason why God sent this testing to Paul: "For this thing I besought the Lord thrice, that it might depart from me. And he said unto me, My grace is sufficient for thee" (vv. 8-9). This thorn was Paul's continuing portion by which God showed forth His sufficiency to Paul and through him. He does not say exactly what the thorn was, but several things in the epistle seem to indicate that it was in the realm of physical weakness. Paul probably made Luke the physician his associate so that Luke could minister to his bodily needs as he traveled from place to place. In writing to the Galatians, Paul said, "See with what large letters I am writing to you" (6:11, NASB), as though in order to see what he was writing he had to write with very large letters. Many feel that the apostle suffered from some serious eye disease which extended over a considerable period of time. That was why he didn't travel alone as he went through the length and breadth of Asia Minor and up and down Greece. He had to have someone to walk along with him because he needed someone to show him the way. This would indicate why it was so serious, for instance, when Paul was in prison, and he said, "All men hath forsaken me" and he exhorted Timothy to come to him quickly. He needed somebody because this was a continuing infirmity. But Paul did not stop because of this weakness of the flesh. When we read the record of his missionary journeys, we don't realize that a man about sixty-five years of age was traveling on foot through mountain passes some 10,000 feet high that are perpetually covered with snow. Travel was most strenuous. He was infirm in body, but he never stopped. There were those who exhorted him to turn the work over to somebody else, but Paul kept right on going. Why? This infirmity was given to show the sufficiency of the grace of God, and Paul continued in spite of his physical infirmity as a testimony to the fact that "my grace is sufficient for thee."

Paul speaks of a third reason that this thorn was given to him: "Most gladly therefore will I rather glory in my infirmities, that the power of Christ may rest upon me" (v. 9). Notice the phrase, "The power of Christ may rest upon me." Then Paul says, "When I am weak, then am I strong" (v. 10b). This infirmity produced a constant and conscious dependence upon God. Paul knew that he could never make it or do it alone. He had to depend upon God.

When Jacob wrestled with the angel all night and the angel touched the hollow of Jacob's thigh so his thigh was out of joint, all Jacob could do to keep fom falling on his face was to hold onto the angel. And when morning came, Jacob was standing there, not in his own strength but supported by the angel. At that point, how strong was Jacob? He was just as strong as the one on whom he leaned, the angel. Paul, an elderly man, was weakened in body and worn out in the Lord's service, yet he was constantly on the go for his Lord. What strength was he operating in? His strength was the strength of the one on whom he was leaning. He had to lean because of his own weakness. A piece of copper wire can be bent and twisted at will; it offers no resistance. If that wire is welded to a piece of railroad track, its strength hasn't been changed one bit; but because it has been joined to the railroad track, it is no longer possible to bend that copper wire. It is the same copper wire—just as weak as ever—but it has been joined to that which is unbendable. That was Paul's experience. Christ's power was his because he had to depend upon Him. What was it that kept him depending? It was the thorn in the flesh. What benefit did Paul find through his suffering? He found that it kept him from pride. It showed him God's sufficiency. It produced a dependence that revealed Christ's power in the apostle's experience.

Job, the blind man, and Paul all suffered, but their sufferings were different. Each learned something different from what they experienced, but all their sufferings were allowed by God in order that He could reveal Himself through the sufferer to those who were witnessing the suffering. Thus the suffering was not only for the benefit of Job and the blind man and Paul, but for the whole generation in which these men lived. It not only did something for the sufferers, but it was for those who beheld the suffering.

In the light of these facts, what should be the attitude of the child of God when he is called on to suffer? Several things are significant. First is Paul's response to suffering: "*Most gladly* therefore will I rather glory in my infirmities, that the power of Christ may rest upon me. Therefore I take pleasure in infirmities, in reproaches, in necessities, in persecutions, in distresses for Christ's sake" (2 Co 12:9-10). Had suffering produced a perverted mental condition in this man which made him say that he welcomed suffering? No, he saw the end. He grasped God's purpose for him in the suffering; and he desired for himself what God desired for him, so he could glory in suffering. The apostle had his eye on the goal: conformity to Christ. Then again Paul has a comforting word: "There hath no temptation [test] taken you but such as is common to man [Now notice these words]: but God is faithful, who will not suffer you to be tempted [or tested] above that [which] ye are able; but will with the temptation also make a way to escape, that ye may be able to bear it" (1 Co 10:13). God is a master craftsman and knows the endurance power of the material with which He is working. God understands His material. He knows when He's working with something that is very fragile and can break easily, and when He's working with something that is tough like flint. Thus God doesn't deal with the fragile as though it were flint, nor does He deal with the flint as though it were fragile glass. That is what Paul meant when he said, "God . . . will not suffer you to be tempted [tested] above that ye are able, but will with the temptation [or testing] also make a way to escape, that ye may be able to bear it" (v. 13b).

God fits the testing to the material at hand. God knows some whom He can trust with a good deal of suffering. He knows others whom He can trust with almost no suffering at all, and God will give us no more than we can be trusted with. Suffering is not punishment, so we cannot say that the greater the sin, the greater the testing. Rather, the more trustworthy the instrument, the heavier the suffering. God is honored or glorified little through the one who suffers little, but He is glorified much through the one with whom He

can trust much suffering. His choicest instruments are those
with whom He trusts the most in the way of testing. A piece
of worthless stone will never be subjected to all of the grind-
ing that goes into putting facets on a diamond. It simply
would not be worth the effort. Some of us have been con-
gratulating ourselves on how little suffering we have had and
have taken delight in the fact. We would do well to ask God
what's wrong with us that we can be trusted with so little,
so that we can bring glory to Himself.

Again, all that God is doing, He is doing to reproduce
Jesus Christ in us. Some of us who have suffered so little will
be just a pen-and-ink line drawing of Jesus Christ. An artist
with a few deft strokes of the pen can reproduce an outline
likeness. But it's a very simple likeness. On the other hand,
the artist may reproduce the person in stone with every detail
delineated. Some of us have suffered so little we reveal only
an outline sketch, and others will reveal the glory of Christ
because of all of the chisel and hammer blows that God has
used to reproduce His image in them. May God give us the
grace first of all to covet that likeness to Christ, then to submit to His discipline so that His image might be reproduced
in us. James learned this because he said, "My brethren,
count it all joy when you fall into divers testings" (1:2).
Joy in testings? Yes, because the testing is the proof that
God sees us as material worth investing effort in to make us
like Christ. May God give us a submissive heart that accepts
God's tests in the light of His purpose to conform us to Christ,
so that His glory is revealed in us.

3

God's Answer to

THE PROBLEM OF
DISAPPOINTMENT

2 KINGS 5:20-27

Do you ever have days when nothing seems to go as you planned? Have you ever gotten up in the morning and thought through the day that was before you and outlined your activities, so you knew exactly what you were going to do? Then you got ready to go to bed at night, did you look back and find out that you hadn't gotten a thing done that you expected to do? That's the story of many a life because it seems as though things seldom go as planned. That is what disappointment is. Disappointment means "not as appointed" or "not as planned." It may take one form for a boy and quite another for his dad. For the boy it may be that picnic that got rained out; things didn't go as he planned. The dad may have expected his boy to mow the lawn, and the rain disappointed him too, because the lawn was still unmowed and had to be done.

Things just don't go as planned. We realize that we're living in an upside-down world, and we wonder sometimes if we can make things come out as we plan or desire. We recognize full well that we are living in an unredeemed body, in an unredeemed creation, with an unredeemed nature within us. So, we may well ask ourselves the question, How is it

37

possible for anything ever to work out right? How can we be
kept from disappointment?

The Word of God has an answer to the problem of disappointment. We would like to make a few suggestions concerning God's answer to disappointment and will divide the
subject into two different areas. The first area is disappointment because of circumstances. In Stephen's address before
the council in reviewing Israel's past history he recounts an
incident in the life of Moses which would have given Moses
abundant cause to be disappointed because circumstances
did not work out as he had expected: "And Moses was
learned in all the wisdom of the Egyptians, and was mighty
in words and in deeds" (Ac 7:22). Moses had been brought
up in pharaoh's court and educated in all the wisdom of the
Egyptians. Evidently he had been made a governmental
administrator and had taken a great deal of the responsibility
off pharaoh's shoulders. He was a man of position, influence
and power among his people and among the Egyptians
among whom he had grown up. "And when he was full forty
years old, it came into his heart to visit his brethren the
children of Israel. And seeing one of them suffer wrong, he
defended him, and avenged him that was oppressed, and
smote the Egyptian" (vv. 23-24). In exerting authority as a
governmental administrator, Moses had killed the Egyptian
who was persecuting an Israelite. He was quite confident
he would be accepted by Israel because he was appearing
on the scene not as a puppet of pharaoh, but rather as a
savior, as a deliverer for those who were downtrodden and
oppressed. But this is where disappointment set in: "For
he supposed his brethren would have understood how that
God by his hand would deliver them: but they understood
not. And the next day he shewed himself unto them as they
strove, and would have set them at one again, saying, Sirs,
ye are brethren; why do ye wrong one to another?" (vv.

25-26). Moses was doing a work of reconciliation by attempting to take two Israelites who were brothers according to their common inheritance and bring them into mutual agreement. He had sought to deliver an Israelite from the Egyptian the day before, and now he was trying to deliver one Israelite from another Israelite. "But he that did his neighbour wrong thrust him away, saying, Who made thee a ruler and a judge over us? Wilt thou kill me, as thou diddest the Egyptian yesterday? Then fled Moses at this saying, and was a stranger in the land of Midian, where he begat two sons" (vv. 27-29).

And he stayed in Midian for forty years. Disappointment! Moses had every reason to be thoroughly and completely dejected because of disappointment. Certainly circumstances did not work out for him as he had anticipated. It had been revealed to Moses that he had been set apart by God as a deliverer, so he sought to use his authority as an administrator in pharaoh's government to accomplish a deliverance. But when he sought to reconcile two brethren, the brethren rejected him, repudiating his rights to act as mediator. They scorned, rebuked, and rejected him, with the result that he had to forsake the office and the influence and wealth that he had in pharaoh's court and take up residence as a shepherd in the backside of the desert.

What a change! what a comedown! He had dwelt in pharaoh's house with all the material comforts and wealth that pharaoh could heap upon him as a trusted administrator. But now he is out tending sheep in the backside of the desert. Moses would certainly conclude that circumstances did not go according to plan, and he might well have been carried away by disappointment. Perhaps we often feel like Moses— our world has collapsed around us and that which we thought God was going to do through us has remained undone. Circumstances have fallen in upon us as the walls of Jericho, and we are caught under them. There is no escape. There's no deliverance, because circumstances are adverse and have caught us in their grip.

What is God's answer to circumstances that are a disappointment? First, we need to recognize that our God is not a God controlled by circumstances, but He is a God who controls circumstances. That is a nontheological way of affirming the great truth that God is sovereign. He rules over all. For example, one of the great prerogatives of God the Son is that He upholds all things by the Word of His power (Heb 1:3). The apostle is speaking of this created universe of which we are but an infinitesimally small part, and he says that this universe is supported or held together by the word of God's power.

The physicist may talk a great deal about gravity, but if you ask him to define or explain gravity he is at a loss to do so. He knows that gravity operates and he can trace the principles by which it operates, but he cannot tell what gravity is. The Word of God tells us that what the scientist calls gravity actually is the word of Christ's power holding all things together. He is in absolute control over all creation, over the created universe, and all that is within the universe; and this God who upholds all things through His Son, by the word of His power, is not a God who is controlled by circumstances, but a God who orders circumstances according to His own perfect will. The psalmist says, "My times are in thy hand: deliver me from the hand of mine enemies, and from them that persecute me. Make thy face to shine upon thy servant: save me for thy mercies' sake. Let me not be ashamed, O LORD" (Ps 31:15-17).

The psalmist is saying that since his times are in God's hand, he is not under the control of circumstances. The God who controls the material earth is also the God who controls time; and the psalmist can say, "My times are in thy hands."

He is not only speaking of duration of life, but he is talking about all that takes place within a span of a man's lifetime, that which comes every moment of every day is in the hand of God. Christ not only upholds by His hand, but all of the circumstances in every moment of our existence are in His hands. Psalm 121 provides another word. Many times God's children have turned to this psalm for comfort and help and have asked the question, "Will I lift up mine eyes unto the hills?" The hills are the most solid, unshakable, immovable things that men know anything about. They seemed to be eternal to the ancient. Therefore, he said, " Will I lift mine eyes into the immovable hills and seek help from those. From whence cometh my help?" Then he replied, "My help cometh from the Lord which made the hills. He made the heaven and the earth." The hills may have seemed timeless to the shepherd who had trodden paths, following the sheep up and down the steeps, but the psalmist recognized the hills were created by a God who founded the hills, and this God is eternal.

> He will not suffer thy foot to be moved: . . . he that keep-eth Israel shall neither slumber nor sleep. The LORD is thy keeper: the LORD is thy shade upon thy right hand. The sun shall not smite thee by day, nor the moon by night. The LORD shall preserve thee from all evil: he shall preserve thy soul. The LORD shall preserve thy going out and thy coming in from this time forth, and even for evermore (Ps 121:3-8).

The psalmist is saying that the God who created, the God who upholds and sustains, is a God who is sovereign over every circumstance in my life. He controls my footsteps. He controls me when I sleep. He gives me shade by day, and protection by night. No evil can harm me. The Lord shall preserve my going out and my coming in. Every circumstance is under His sovereign control. So the first great affirmation that we make as God's answer to disappointment is this revelation from the Word that God is sovereign and in control over all circumstances in life.

The second thing that the Word of God had to say is that, since God is sovereign, He has a plan for each one of His children. Our God is an infinite God, and this is where our comprehension fails us because so often we are distracted by the multiplicity of details that we are called upon to meet. We get frustrated by them. For example, a housewife is in the kitchen, trying to get dinner ready, and her husband is sitting in the den reading his paper. Over the top of the paper he calls out, "When is supper going to be ready?" Then their youngster comes along and pleads, "Mommy, do this. It's got to be done right now!" Just then the telephone at her elbow rings, and another child cries out and demands his mother's help. The housewife is absolutely frustrated because she cannot give her attention to all of these demands at the same time. We in our frustration and disappointment bring God down to our frustrated level, and we wonder if things get too much for God and out of His control so that He throws up His hands and says, "I quit. You look out for yourself." But our God is an infinite God and, as an infinite God, can give His infinite attention to an infinite number of details at any one time. God is as vitally concerned about each fleeting moment in your life and the circumstances that press in upon you in it as though you were the only child that He had to watch out for. God is not only sovereign, He is infinite. And as an infinite, sovereign God, all details are ordered according to His perfect plan.

It is impossible for us to see as God sees because we look at our circumstances which are like an enveloping cloud that surrounds us, preventing us from seeing outside them. There's a vast difference between being on the ground when a thundercloud is overhead and being in a jet plane above the storm. What a different viewpoint you get when you are looking down on it from when you are looking up at it. Things that disappoint us are disappointments because we cannot discern God's plan and distinguish the movements of His hands. We are disappointed because we have set up our plan and are moving according to our appointment. When our plans or our appointments collapse, then our whole world crashes in upon us. When we substitute our plan for God's will or plan we can be certain that we will be carried away by disappointment because of circumstances. The child of God who has learned to find and then follow God's will is one who can be delivered from disappointment because of circumstances. If a rain cloud comes when he has planned a picnic, he says, "This must be God's perfect will for me," and accepts it as such; and if the sun shines, he accepts that as God's will and rejoices in it and praises God for it. When a man says, "This is what I will do, this is the way I will spend my day, this is the way I will invest my time and my money" and then sees things going astray, he can't help but be disappointed and defeated because his plan has been substituted for God's plan. Fortunately God does not consult us as to what our will is and then conform to it. If God did that, we would have no disappointments; but who knows what it would be like if we tried to plot out our own plan. Fortunately God doesn't consult us. He tells us as an infinite, wise, loving, and sovereign God what His plan and His will are, and deliverance from disappointment because of circumstances comes from being rightly adjusted to God's will since He is sovereign and infinite and has a perfect plan. Our disappointments are God's appointments to accomplish His perfect will in us.

A second area in which we find disappointment is in people. Perhaps this is more trying than the first. Somehow we seem to be able to adjust to changing circumstances, but

many times we have to face disappointment because we feel
that people have failed us. Scripture records many failures
of men who brought disappointments to those who trusted
in them. Think of the experience of Moses, for instance,
when he stood trembling before God and asked for someone
to stand with him. God set Aaron apart, and said, "Aaron
will be to you instead of a mouth." And Moses and Aaron
were those whom God used in the administration of the camp
of Israel. In Exodus 24 God took Moses up into the mount
in order that He might reveal Himself and His law, and
Aaron was left at the foot of the mountain. When Moses
came down from the mount he heard a great shout going up
from the camp of Israel, and as he drew near he found that
Israel had been led to make a golden calf which they named
"the God which had led them out of Egypt." Who led Israel
in making the calf? Aaron. Disappointment in a person. In
Numbers 12, Miriam and Aaron spake against Moses because
of the Ethiopian woman whom he had married from among
the Semites from the Arab country where Moses had so-
journed during the forty years he was in the wilderness.
Moses' leadership is questioned. His authority is jeopardized,
as these two are claiming equal authority along with Moses.
They say, "Hath the LORD indeed spoken only by Moses?
Hath he not spoken also by us?" (v. 2). Who were the two
that brought such disappointment to Moses? Miriam and
Aaron. Those who were closest to him after the flesh had
failed him.

In 2 Kings 5, Elisha, the man of God, had a trusted servant,
Gehazi, who was being groomed by the prophet to take his
place even as he had been groomed by Elijah to take his
place. This was to have been the succession: Elijah—Elisha—
Gehazi. And as Elijah had trained Elisha, so Elisha trained
Gehazi to be God's man to succeed him as God's mouthpiece.
But after the miracle in which God manifested His mercy to

Naaman and granted him physical cleanness, covetousness crept into Gehazi's heart. He went out to meet Naaman, and lied. He asked Naaman to give him money and clothes for two of God's poor prophets. His story touched Naaman's heart and he received what he asked. After he had gone home and hid that which he had gotten by deception, he came into the house of his teacher, master, and companion. Elisha said, "Whence comest thou?" He said, "Thy servant went no whither." Elisha knew the whole story. Do you think he was disappointed? Of course he was; this one in whom he had invested so much time and effort and training turned out to be unworthy of the privileges of being God's spokesman.

In Acts 15 Paul and Barnabas desired to go and visit the churches that they had established. "And Barnabas determined to take with them John, whose surname was Mark. But Paul thought not good to take him with them, who departed from them from Pamphylia, and went not with them to the work" (15:37-38). Why not? Because Paul had been disappointed in John Mark and had lost confidence in him and left him behind. In 2 Timothy 4:10 Paul mentions that "Demas hath forsaken me, having loved this present world." Disappointment! We can go from the beginning to the end of Scripture and find it abounds with references to men who were disappointed in people as well as disappointed in circumstances. If there were anyone who had a right to be disappointed in men, it was our Lord. In John 6, after our Lord fed the multitude with bread, He very carefully explained to them that He had not come to fill their bellies with material bread, but He had come to fill their hearts and souls with the bread of heaven and that they must partake of Him. John records that from that time on many of His disciples forsook Him and walked no more with Him. After receiving benefits, blessings, and instructions from the Lord, they turned away. He had a right to be disappointed. He chose twelve and knew that one of them would take the place of an accusing witness against Him and would betray Him, selling Him for thirty pieces of silver. He had a right to be disappointed in Judas. Peter denied Him. He had a right to be disappointed in Peter.

However, nothing in the gospels indicates that Christ was ever disappointed in man—in spite of all the provocations. If we can find out what kept Christ from being disappointed in people, I believe it will help us and give us the clue to how to keep from being disappointed in people. The answer is: "Jesus did not commit himself unto them, because he knew all men, and needed not that any should testify of man: for he knew what was in man" (Jn 2:24-25). That passage of Scripture reveals that Jesus Christ was not disappointed in man because He did not expect from men that which He knew they could not perform or fulfill. In other words, our Lord knew the propensity of evil in the heart of men and, knowing that, He was never taken by surprise when men did that which He knew all the time was their nature and character.

This tells us that we live by a double standard. We expect of men what we do not hold ourselves responsible for; and if we committed the same failures that disappoint us in others, we would excuse ourselves. But because somebody else does it we hold them responsible and we're swept away by disappointment. Our Lord knew exactly what was in man; and because He knew, He did not have a higher standard for them than it was possible for them to attain. In the upper room when the Lord revealed that one of the twelve would betray Him, each man in turn, right around the table, asked Him the question, "Lord, is it I?" "I couldn't be the one, could I?" And each man at that moment saw in himself the possibility of doing what Judas ultimately did. Those men would not at that point have been disappointed in Judas because they realized that each one of them could have done that very thing, were circumstances so arranged. Recognizing this possibility, not one of them spoke a reproachful word when it was revealed that Judas was the one, because each saw the capability within himself of doing it. Later when our Lord said that they all should flee and abandon Him, they all affirmed, "Not I, Lord. I couldn't possibly do that." Because they did not see the possibility in themselves for doing that, when Peter did it they were swept away with disappointment in him.

Do you see the difference? Not only do we have a sovereign God who has an infinite plan, who can control circumstances, who can deliver us from disappointment because of circumstances, but we must have a correct view of man and not think of him more highly than we ought to think. Romans 12:3 says no man should "think of himself more highly than he ought to think." But if you would keep from being disappointed in others, then you must not hold someone else responsible for a higher standard than you hold for yourself. This is where the problem arises, for the Word of God does not hold us responsible for the standards we can attain but for those we can't attain. The Word of God says, "Be ye holy, for I am holy." We recognize God's standard and put ourselves in the position of judges and sit as judges of another man's life. In elevating ourselves to that position, we begin to condemn another man, and then disappointment sweeps us away. We need a correct view of God lest we be swept away by circumstances, and a correct view of what man is with all of his capacities and propensities for evil, lest we be completely swept away by what man is. The believer possesses two capacities or natures—the old, which is corrupt, sinful, and evil; and the new, which is the nature of Christ imparted to us. When we fail to recognize that the saint of

God has these two capacities, we will continue to be disappointed by man's failures.

The saints of God—Moses, Elisha, the apostle Paul—who were disappointed in men, always had to turn to God when they were conscious of men's failures. We sometimes feel that those who have been saved and have been set apart to become the Lord's servants, those whom the Lord uses in one way or another, have lost all capacity to sin. We think that they feel differently, react differently, act differently. I heard recently of a little girl who, in talking to her pastor, said, "Pastor, you know, it's hard for me to believe that you are people." So many of us have that view of God's children. We fail to recognize the same disappointment, the same discouragement, the same likes and dislikes, the same hurts, the same responses. How easy it is to get our eyes on men and their failure and lose sight of Jesus Christ.

There is another clue to the answer of the problem of disappointment in people. "Wherefore seeing we also are compassed about with so great a cloud of witnesses, let us lay aside every weight, and the sin which doth so easily beset us, and let us run with patience the race that is set before us, Looking unto Jesus the author and finisher of our faith" (Heb 12:1-2). When you are running a race, it is imperative to keep your eye on the goal—not on the other contestants, not on the course, but on the goal. It is the Spirit's ministry to reveal Jesus Christ to us and to set Him before us as the goal toward which we run. The contestant who diverts his eye from Christ and becomes occupied with people is soon going to stumble in disappointment. People were not given as models for others to follow; that prerogative belongs to Christ. You may have the best Sunday school teacher who ever taught, but that teacher should not be your model. You may remember a faithful pastor, but he should not be your model. You may have a godly parent, but that parent should not be your model. The pattern is the Lord; and when you get your eyes off Him and begin to look at a person, sooner or later you will be disappointed in that person and will be swept away. Recognizing what is in man, it becomes imperative that we look only unto Jesus, "the author and finisher of our faith; who for the joy that was set before him endured the cross, despising the shame, and is set down on the right hand of the throne of God" (Heb 12:2).

Basically our solution to the problem of disappointment through circumstances or disappointment in people is the same; it is wrapped up in that one phrase: "Looking unto Jesus." Circumstances are in His control. Therefore, in circumstances, look unto Him. He has been revealed as the way, the truth, and the life. The way that we should walk is in Him. The truth that we should conform to is in Him. The life that we should live is in Him. Not to people do we look but to the altogether lovely one. When your heart is dejected because of disappointment, whether of circumstances or from people, look unto Jesus because He is the Sovereign God who is ordering all things according to His perfect will, and in Him is all perfection. There is no failure. Therefore, there can be no disappointment. If you would live without disappointment, "Turn your eyes upon Jesus. Look full in His wonderful face. And the things of earth [with all of their disappointments and discouragements] will grow strangely dim, in the light of His glory and grace."

4

God's Answer to

THE PROBLEM OF WORRY

MATTHEW 6:25-34

Not too long ago I was in a home where the son had just become married. The parents with whom I was visiting discussed the changed situation in that home. It was hard for them to go to bed at night and not keep one ear tuned to hear the door slam or the garage door close. They no longer waited for him to come to meals. Life had changed for them and they were not yet adjusted to it. The mother became a little wistful at the thought that her boy was gone, and her husband turned to her and said, "But now your worries are over." She replied, "Yes, dear, but you know I'm not happy unless I'm worrying."

Many of us would in one way or another testify to that same fact. Worry seems to be an integral part of living, and if we live we worry. One cannot pick up the newspaper from day to day without realizing that we have a great deal about which we ought to be worrying. We all have been told we shouldn't worry, but there is every reason why we should worry—if God is dead, and if the Bible is not to be trusted, and if we do not have a heavenly Father who watches over us personally and has assumed responsibility for us. If those things are not true, we had better worry. But because we do have a heavenly Father who has a predetermined plan and purpose for each one of His children, who has assumed responsibility for our food, provision, protection, and care, and who can distinguish each bird in the heavens and each blade of grass in the fields, then we ought to ask ourselves the question: Why worry?

In dealing with this problem of God's answer for worry, at the outset we ought to face the fact honestly that worry, according to the Word of God, is a sin. It is not dealt with as a weakness or a failure that is excused because everyone worries. Worry is dealt with as a sin. Any commandment that God gives that is not obeyed is a sin. It is striking that whenever there is a reference to worry in the Bible, it is cast in the terms of a command. For instance in Matthew 6:25 our Lord said, "Take no thought for your life." Putting that in the simplest terms, He said, "Don't worry. Stop giving way to anxious care." In the original text His words are in the form of a command to His children. Furthermore, when God's Word deals with the problem of worry it always deals with it in the relationship of worry and the believer. Nothing deals with the problem of worry in an unbeliever because, as suggested earlier, there is every reason why an unbeliever should give way to anxious care. But in speaking to His disciples who had acknowledged Him as Saviour, Christ gave the commandment, "Take no thought, do not give way to anxious care concerning your life." Or again, He said, "Let not your heart be troubled" (Jn 14:1). That was a command. The Lord recognized that they were troubled, and He told them to stop worrying; it was wrong for them to give way to anxiety and crippling fear. He did not give an exhortation: "Children, it would be nice if you wouldn't. Won't you please stop?" He gave a command: "Don't."

The apostle Paul, in dealing with that same subject, said, "Be careful [anxious] for nothing" (Phil 4:6). Once again the apostle did not give an exhortation as he did on so many occasions. He gave a specific command: "Don't worry about anything." Peter, in speaking of the same problem, said, "Casting all your care upon him; for he careth for you" (1 Pe 5:7). The word *care* means anxiety or "anxious care." Peter, like his predecessors that we cited, was not giving an exhortation but rather a command. The things that are exhorted are in the realm where the child of God may or may not respond. True, if an exhortation is given he ought to respond, but no necessary compulsion is attached. But when a command is given in the Bible, there is no option in the matter; it is not for us to decide whether we will or won't. If we are to be the sons of God without rebuke, if we are to manifest the image of Jesus Christ, and if we are to be conformed to His image, then we must obey the commands put before us. When God gives a specific commmand to His child and that command is not fulfilled, the child of God has sinned in disobedience. Thus we must first of all honestly face this fact that when we give way to worry, anxious care, and concern, we are disobeying a specific command of Scripture given by God to His children, and we are displeasing Him because of our sin.

Not many believers ever feel constrained in the light of the convicting work of God's Spirit to use 1 John 1:9 concerning their worry. If we believers confess our sins, "he is faithful and just to forgive us our sins, and to cleanse us from all unrighteousness." If we fall into some sin and are convicted by the Holy Spirit, we quickly turn to that verse and claim its promise. We become specific about the sin we have committed and confess it before the Lord so that fellowship might be restored. But if we were to be honest, not many of us have ever said to God, "I worried today. That worry was a sin. It broke my fellowship. I'm confessing it so that I might be restored." If this is a sin as the Word says it is, and we fall into it—and we all do—then this is a matter that must be confessed if we are to maintain fellowship with the Father.

Then we might ask ourselves, What do you mean by worry? Does that mean that a father is not to assume responsibilities for his household? Is he not to look ahead and plan for their needs? Is he not to plan ahead in his business? Is he not to make provision for those bills that must be met the first of next month? Is he to let them take care of themselves when they come? Is that what it means when it says "don't worry"? Scripture says that he that doesn't provide for his own house is worse than an infidel, and further, it says that we as children of light are to be as wise as children of darkness in use of material things and use them wisely as an investment for God. Where do we draw the line between careful planning for our needs and the needs of our families and worry and care that is forbidden by the Word of God?

In the light of the Lord's teaching in Matthew 6:25 and in John 14:1 and Paul's teaching in Philippians 4:6, worry is the anxious care that comes from assuming a responsibility which we are incapable of discharging. If I knew that I were going to have to buy a six-cent postage stamp to mail a letter tomorrow, it wouldn't particularly bother me because I happen to have that much change in my pocket right now. Thus, I have a reasonable expectation of meeting that obligation and would have no worry. But suppose my church board should decide it was my obligation to pay off the indebtedness of our church tomorrow. If I assumed the responsibility of discharging that note tomorrow morning, I would have anxious care because I would be utterly incapable of discharging that debt. In His command Christ was not talking about meeting that which we are responsible to meet, because that is our God-given responsibility. He was talking about assuming somebody else's responsibility, namely, God's responsibility which we ourselves cannot assume because we cannot take His place. When we make His responsibility our responsibility we find that we have assumed a crushing weight that we are incapable of discharging. Only God knows how many of His children have been broken because they were not willing to let God be God and to let Him fulfill that which He has assumed as His responsibility for us. We have assumed that responsibility which He never put upon us; and we have been broken in body, health, mind, strength, and energy because we have not fulfilled the command to leave the things of God to God and to assume only those things that God in His will has entrusted to us with our limited capacity.

In Matthew 6:25 are two principal areas in which the individual will assume a responsibility which he himself cannot discharge. First of all, it has to do with material things: "Take no thought for your life, what ye shall eat, or what ye shall drink." And the second area is in the area of the body on physical health: "nor yet for your body, what ye shall put on." Notice that Christ made no reference to spiritual things. Since the sinner can contribute nothing toward his salvation, and the child of God depends upon the Father's faithfulness to sustain him in the salvation provided in Christ, the area of spiritual things is left out of the Lord's consideration. But He recognizes two areas in which men will succumb to gnawing anxiety and concern. First, about the material things in this life. When He says, "what ye shall eat, or what ye shall drink," He is speaking of the broad area of material things which men value so much: the bank account, financial investments, the furnishings for our home, the material comforts we can enjoy. A man may so attach himself to these things that he finds himself crushed by what he does not have rather than by what he has. The second area is the unnatural anxiety or concern concerning the body: how it will be sustained, how it will be preserved and protected, how to ward off this weakness and that infirmity or disease. So Christ, dealing with areas in which His disciples had particular problems, put a finger on that which brings so much anxiety and concern to men today: their material things and their physical well-being.

In this study, the causes of worry are not as important as the scriptural antidotes, although in dealing with the antidotes of worry we have to deal somewhat with the causes as well. In the light of several passages in the Word of God there seem to be three parts to God's answer for worry. First, Christ said, "Let not your heart be troubled . . ." or given over to anxious care (Jn 14:1). Stop and think a moment. There was every reason they should have worried from the human standpoint. For three and one-half years the one who had summoned them to Himself had supplied their every need. Previously they had been independent, self-sustaining businessmen. But they had been called out of the business world, and now they had no means of support. Yet, our Lord had provided for them. They hadn't missed a meal. They had had clothing provided for them; they had been sheltered, guided, and directed—everything they needed the Lord had supplied. Now He had been telling them that He was going away, and the thought began to dawn on them that He who had provided for and cared for them would no longer be with them. They concluded that He would not continue to supply their need any longer, and they said, "We are just like orphaned children."

Christ understood their feeling because He said, "I will not leave you comfortless" (Jn 14:18), which literally means "I will not leave you orphaned." Knowing their anxious care for the material necessities of life, Christ was aware that they had succumbed to spiritual heart trouble—worry and anxiety. Yet, He recognized why their anxiety had come, so He gave them what is the first antidote to any worry, no matter what the cause: "Ye believe in God, believe also in me." Faith is the antidote to worry. In Matthew 6:26 the Lord shows how

foolish it is for a man to worry when he has a heavenly
Father: "Behold the fowls of the air." How did they get
there? God created them. God's relationship to the birds is
a relationship of Creator to creature. That's an impersonal
relationship rather than a personal one. But what does the
Creator do for His creation? He feeds them. The Creator
feeds the birds. What were the disciples worried about?
That they wouldn't have food to eat at the next meal. That's
what they were worried about in John 14. Jesus said, "Now
wait a minute. Just think of what I taught you before. If
God the Creator takes care of an insignificant bird in His
creation, do you think the one who has this close, personal
relationship to you as Father will forget His children? If
God the Creator can't forget a bird to whom He has an impersonal relationship, do you think He can forget a son with
whom He has a personal relationship? So why worry?"

Then He continues: "Why take ye thought for raiment?
Consider the lilies of the field, how they grow; they toil not,
neither do they spin: and yet I say unto you, That even
Solomon in all his glory was not arrayed like one of these"
(vv. 28-29). Who arrayed the lily? God did. The applica-
tion is: "If God so clothe the grass of the field . . . shall he
not much more clothe you, O ye of little faith?" (v. 30).
What characterizes these disciples given over to anxious care
in this passage? They had little faith. The antidote to worry
was to trust God, because God knew every need of every
bird. Furthermore, He knew the need of each individual
blade of grass in the field; and God the Creator was faithful
to His creation and saw that its need was supplied. If God
will do that for His creation will He not do that for His sons?
So Christ was showing that the antidote to worry is to let
God be God. And if God has declared in the Word that He
assumes a certain responsibility, we are asked to believe that
God is a gentlemen and will fulfill what He has promised.

Imagine that you have some physical or material need. You begin to wring your hands and give way to anxious care as to how that need is going to be met. What you are saying by your actions is, "I believe that God is a liar, and I believe that He will forget me or fail me." We believe that we will be the first ones in all the history of creation that God has ever failed. No one else has ever testified that God failed him, but we somehow feel that we will be the first ones. The only basis for disbelief and worry about that which God has promised is to say, "God is not faithful to His word," and He will not fulfill what He has promised.

In the same passage Christ shows the fruitlessness of worry. He says, in effect, "What good will worry do you? By worrying can you increase your stature one cubit?" (v. 27). Worry accomplishes nothing, except to destroy the worrier; consequently, it is profitless. Then He points out that God knows the need and is not ignorant of our lack. "Your heavenly Father knoweth that ye have need of all these things" (v. 32). Somehow we feel that we have to worry because God is ignorant of our need. It goes back to this concept: Just how big of a God do you have? We are so constructed that we can give attention to only one thing at any one point of time. So we have pulled God down to our level and are convinced that He is no bigger than we are; therefore, we reason, He can't give His attention to any more things at one time than we can. If he is giving attention to your need, obviously He can't be occupied with mine. Let God be God. What kind of a God is He? An infinite God, He can give His infinite attention to an infinite number of things at any one moment of time. If we believe that is the kind of God we have, then we have the assurance that He can give as detailed and individual attention to us and our needs, as though we were the only child that He had to look

after. "Your heavenly Father knoweth that ye have need of
all these things." He will take care of them.

In instructing the disciples concerning that which He
recognized as a very prevalent need, Christ pointed out that
the child of God needs to trust the Father to do what He
said He would do. Obviously, before we can be delivered
from worry and begin to trust God to do what He promised,
we have to know what it was He promised. That brings us
back to God's Word. Many of us worry because we don't
have the faintest idea of the obligations that God has actually
assumed. We don't know what God's work is and what He
has promised to do because we've never gone through the
Bible to see what He has said He would do for His children.
It is proverbial that the last thing one does when he buys an
appliance is read the directions. Only after one experiments
with it, trying to see how it works, does he consult the instructions to see how it operates. We are no different with
the Word of God. We fall into worry, giving way to anxious
care that cripples us emotionally and physically. Although
God has a specific set of directions and has told us exactly
what He would do if we would believe Him, we don't know
that we can lay hold of God because we are ignorant of the
Word. We don't know what He has promised to do for us.

I have a homeowner's insurance policy. I really don't know
what it covers. Six panes of glass were cracked by some
neighborhood boys, and I keep wondering whether the insurance will take care of those. But I haven't bothered to look
up my policy to see whether that is covered. If I have a need
that God has promised to meet which He has covered in a
blanket policy and I don't know enough about that policy He
has given me to lay claim on Him, I may gnaw away with
worry and care out of sheer ignorance. We can't trust a God
of whom we are ignorant. And before we can be delivered
from worry we must know Him and become aware of what

He has promised to do. Thus the Lord's first antidote to worry is to trust, to believe, and to claim the promises.

A second antidote to worry is in 1 Peter 5:7: "Casting all your care [worries] upon him; for he careth [worries] for you." Peter used the same word concerning our care and God's care for us. If God is exercising watchful care over us it is pointless for us at the same time to be given over to anxious care. Peter says, "Casting all your care upon him . . ." Note that word *casting*. It means to turn over to somebody else. Take your hands off it and let somebody else bear it for you. The psalmist has this same thought when he says, "Cast thy burden on the LORD, and he shall sustain thee" (Ps 55:22). I think we've missed a very precious truth here, because to us the word *cast* suggests picking something up and throwing it. If your worries are insignificant, perhaps you can do that; but if you're experiencing the kind of worries that we are talking about—those that really crush you and break you—they are too heavy for you to pick up and throw anyplace. They press on you, and you feel as though you're going to cave in under their weight. How do you get rid of those things? The psalmist is using the word which means, to roll or to roll off.

Suppose I am supporting a heavy weight on my shoulder that is so heavy that it makes my knees buckle and my back ache. Does that weight stay there by itself? Not on your life. It stays there because I have a firm grip on it and hold it there. What do I have to do to get rid of it? All I have to do is to relax my grip, and the natural force of gravity will make that weight roll off. That is what the psalmist meant: Roll thy burden on the Lord, and He shall sustain thee. When Peter says to cast all your care upon Him, he is talking about a definite act of committal in which the child of God says to his Father, "I've been bearing this thing. But I won't bear it any longer. I'll release my grip on it and let it roll

away so that it will fall off my shoulder onto You." Before
you can keep a burden, you have to get a firm grip on it or it
will fall from you. Did you ever realize that? It is like carrying a basketball on your head—take your hands off, and down
it will go. Your worry stays there because you hold onto it.
But if you are just willing to relax your grip on it and let it
roll on the Lord, then you will find that He will sustain you.
"Casting all your care on him." This is the second antidote to
worry. There must be a specific committal to the Lord of that
which is our worry. We must relax our grip on it so that it
can roll off on Him.

We used to sing the song, "Take your burdens to the Lord
and. . . ." Do what? "Leave them there." Most people act as
though it said, "Take your burdens to the Lord and pick them
up again." That is our practice. That casting of them on the
Lord and walking away and leaving them behind is the act
of casting or committal that Peter is talking about. The
writer of that song was pastor of the largest church in Phila-
delphia. His son, who had an operatic tenor voice, was in
Dallas on one occasion; and Dr. Chafer, president of the
Dallas Theological Seminary, asked him to sing his father's
song in chapel. When he had finished singing, "Take your
burdens to the Lord and leave them there," he leaned over
and said, "And forget all about them." That's what Peter is
talking about. Cast your burdens on the Lord and forget
about them. "Casting your care upon him, for he careth for
you."

There is a third antidote mentioned by the apostle Paul in
Philippians 4:6. Coupled with the command, "Be careful for
nothing," it is: "but in every thing by prayer and supplication
with thanksgiving let your requests be made known unto
God." Our request, according to verse 6, was concerning a
need about which we were worrying. Paul says the antidote
to this anxious care is prayer and supplication. This is not

essentially different from 1 Peter 5:7. But Paul gives us the method by which the child of God commits his burden to the Lord, while Peter gives the means by which he casts his burden on the Lord. Paul tells God his request and then asks God specifically to do something about the need that caused the care in his heart: "Be careful for nothing; but in everything by prayer and supplication with thanksgiving let your requests be made known unto God. And the peace of God, which passeth all understanding, shall keep [do guard duty over] your hearts and minds through Christ Jesus." Peace is that which settles upon a mind guarded by Christ. The mind over which Christ stands sentry duty cannot give way to gnawing anxiety or worry. So, if we would have Him stand guard duty over our minds to resist worry, as we recognize each need, we must present it to our heavenly Father who is able to meet it. We trust Him to do it, and we walk away from the committal with a confidence that God who has heard will supply the need.

How simple this is made in the Word of God. It is not difficult to grasp these simple facts. God knows our needs and has the power to provide them. He will meet our needs as we trust Him and ask Him to do it. He invites us to come with anything that gives anxious care, let it roll off on Him, and He'll put His hand under and bear it when we relax our hold on it. Could anything be any simpler? Yet, many of us have given way to the anxious care forbidden in the Bible because we have not followed the simple procedure of committing our way to Him, expecting Him to meet our need because He is our Father.

If we are to make this practical, we are going to have to begin practicing it. We are well practiced on how to worry but not on how to trust. The next time that anxious care comes and you realize you are getting frustrated and concerned, it's time to stop and say, "I have to commit this to the

Lord. I must release my grip and let it fall off on Him, counting His word as that of a gentleman that He will meet this need." How long does it take to say "Father, I realize I have a need. I am trusting You to do something about it"? That's all it takes. But the worry disappears because He is bearing it for you. We must develop this attitude of quiet confidence that God will meet our needs because He knows them. When He is trusted, He will act. The sign says: "Why trust when you can worry?" And we smile in amusement because worry seems to necessary, so inevitable. But why worry when you can trust an infinite Father to provide for the needs of His children? Nothing would break my heart more than to see one of my girls worry and doubt my word after she had told me of some need and I had said I would take care of it. How many times we've broken the Father's heart when He's told us He would take care of us and we have acted as though we didn't believe Him and have worried instead of trusting.

5

God's Answer to
THE PROBLEM OF DOUBT

JOHN 20:19-29

The Word of God is very frank in recording the lives of those who crossed the pages of the sacred book. Not only are the triumphs, victories and successes of God's saints recorded, but their failures as well. What James said of Elijah could be said of many believers whose lives are recorded in Scripture: "Elias was a man subject to like passions as we" (Ja 5:17). Often we feel that the saints of the Bible must have lived in an entirely different world. Sometimes we imagine that they didn't face the same problems, circumstances, disappointments, heartaches, and burdens that we face. But in examining the record more closely, it is evident that they faced the same practical problems that confront us in day-to-day living.

When we get to heaven and circulate to meet some of the saints, we'll approach Thomas, shake his hand, and say, "So you are doubting Thomas!" We have become so accustomed to thinking of him by the dual term "doubting Thomas" that even in glory we'll probably be unable to disassociate him from his doubts as recorded in John 20. This record of Thomas' reaction to the story of the resurrection casts light on our problems of doubt today.

First, look at the record. It was at the close of a long and trying day. Those women who first came to the tomb were told by the angels that Jesus was no longer there, that He had risen from the dead. Then the angels sent the women into the city to tell the disciples that Christ had arisen from the dead even as He said. That began a hasty trek from the city to the garden and back to the city as the disciples spent the day examining the evidence in the empty tomb. They went to see for themselves that the seal had been broken, the stone had been rolled away, and the tomb in which the body had been placed was now empty. They were satisfied that the wrappings they found were the actual ones that had covered the Lord's body. At the end of the day, the disciples secreted themselves behind barred doors because of fear of the Jews. The Lord had prepared them for the world's animosity and the religious leaders' hatred that they would receive because they were His. He had told them that the world would continue its hatred of Him by venting that hatred against His disciples (Jn 15-16). Fear was very real to them. They were like fearful cowards hiding behind bolted and barred doors. But suddenly their fear was dispelled by the personal presence of the Lord Jesus Christ: "Then the same day at evening, being the first day of the week, when the doors were shut where the disciples were assembled for fear of the Jews, came Jesus and stood in the midst, and saith unto them, Peace be unto you" (Jn 20:19).

Often reference is made to Christ passing through closed doors. Notice that the Scriptures do not reveal how He entered the room. He simply appeared there before them. He materialized in their presence. His resurrected, glorified body was not limited by either time nor space, and He could appear in their midst. The Scriptures make no effort to explain how He came, but they do record the fact that He came. The first thing that Christ did when He appeared in their midst was to pronounce a blessing upon them: "Peace be unto you." It was not strange to the disciples' ears because they had heard it before. In the upper room, shortly before His death, Christ had promised them His peace: "Peace I leave with you, my peace I give unto you: not as the world giveth, give I unto you [for the world can only give fear]. Let not your heart be troubled, neither let it be afraid" (Jn 14:27). The disciples could think back to their experience on the stormy sea when Christ came walking upon the water to them, and He spoke one word: "Peace." Then tranquillity came to the scene. The storm had subsided on the sea and now the storm subsided in their hearts because Jesus Christ had come and pronounced a benediction. This benediction was the first proof the disciples had that this was the same man with whom they had walked for more than three years. This was the first word that many of these disciples heard after His resurrection; and it was a word of comfort, of blessing, and of consolation. When Christ pronounced the word, "Peace," they recognized Him immediately.

Second, notice that Christ identified Himself by His hands and side: "And when he had so said, he shewed unto them his hands and his side" (Jn 20:20). First He was recognized by His voice that pronounced peace and brought blessing. Second, he was identified by what they saw with their eyes, for they looked upon His hands that had been pierced by the nails. They looked upon the side riven by the spear thrust of the Roman soldier. These identifying marks certified that this was not another person, nor was it Christ appearing in another body, but this was truly the resurrected Christ standing in their midst. It is significant that God saw fit to retain in Christ's resurrected body the marks of the nails and spear. I firmly believe that these are the only scars that will be retained in glory. Even though God will remove all scars and signs of the curse which we bear in these bodies, He had seen fit to retain in the resurrected, glorified body of Jesus Christ the nail prints in His hands and feet and the scar from

the spear in His side so that every time we look upon Him in
glory those wounds will remind us how we came home to the
Father's house.

Christ was identified in the third place by a manifestation
of His authority: "As my Father hath sent me, even so send I
you" (20:21). God had sent the Son that He might reveal
the Father to men who were in darkness and ignorance. And
the Son in turn was sending the disciples to men who were in
darkness and ignorance to bring the light of the gospel to
them. When He said this, "he breathed on them, and saith
unto them, Receive ye the Holy Ghost" (v. 22). He had told
them that when He ascended to the Father, He would ask
the Father that the Father might give a gift to them, the
gift of the Spirit; and in anticipation of the Spirit's coming
on the day of Pentecost, they were receiving a foretaste of
the gift that would be given to the world. "Whose soever
sins ye remit, they are remitted unto them; and whose soever
sins ye retain, they are retained" (v. 23).

When Christ confronted the paralytic He said to Him:
"Son, thy sins be forgiven" (Mk 2:5). Immediately He per-
ceived that the religious leaders were challenging His statement and reasoning that only God could forgive sins. Ac-
knowledging that this was true, Christ said that in order that
they might know that the Son of man had power on earth
to forgive sins, He would say to the paralytic, "Arise and
walk," and perform the miracle of healing his body.

Now in that closed room He, who could forgive the sins
of men, gave authority to His disciples to make a judicial pro-
nouncement that those who would come to Him and receive
life from Him would have forgiveness of sins, and those who
would reject that witness and reject Christ as a personal
Saviour would continue under condemnation. The power to
forgive sins resided in the Son of God, but those who were
His representatives could declare His message and assure

men that they had been saved by faith in Him. Before the
ten, Jesus Christ authenticated Himself by His voice pro-
nouncing a blessing, by His hands and feet and side, the retained scars of His wounds, and by the conferral of authority
as His representatives to perform a witness before men.

Thomas, one of the twelve, was not present with the ten.
Scripture makes no explanation as to his absence. Nor does
it tell where he was hiding and why he was not seeking consolation with the ten or seeking security with them from the
Jews. When Thomas returned, he heard the good news that
Jesus had appeared and had fellowshiped with them. "Thomas
. . . called Didymus, was not with them when Jesus came.
The other disciples therefore said unto him, We have seen
the Lord" (Jn 20:24-25a). There must have been a babble
of voices as each of the ten tried to speak louder than the
others to tell Thomas that the Lord had been raised from the
dead and had come and talked with them and blessed them.
I imagine Peter spoke out in a deep bass voice as he thun-
dered out, "The Lord has come!" John, perhaps in more of a
tenor voice, was trying to override Peter's bass as he said,
"Thomas, the Lord has come, and we saw Him." And all the
others began to add their notes to the chorus until Thomas
must have looked around in amazement and wonder. They
had anticipated that he would burst forth in praise and
thanksgiving with them. But instead of rejoicing, they met a
stony wall of doubt. Think of it. Ten bona fide witnesses—
all of whom had seen the same thing and had heard the same
words—gave the identical report; and yet their witness was
not believed. Can you imagine a lawyer having a better
case? Ten witnesses gave a testimony that agreed in every
detail. A lawyer with a case that good would probably try to
change it a bit so it wouldn't look as though there were col-
lusion among the witnesses. Yet, Thomas' reply to their good
news was: "Except I shall see in his hands the print of the

nails, and put my finger into the print of the nails, and thrust my hand into his side, I will not believe" (v. 25b).

"I will not believe." Thomas was saying that he could not and would not accept the evidence presented because his mind and senses were greater authority than the combined testimony of all ten disciples. Thus He trusted and relied upon his mind rather than on what the ten reported.

Thomas' doubt came first of all in spite of the testimony and the evidence of these witnesses. It was not that the case was unsupported nor unsupportable. He willfully and deliberately chose to discredit their testimony. Doubt has to begin with the willful rejection of the evidence presented. When God makes an affirmation and one responds to it in doubt and unbelief, he's saying in effect, "I don't believe what God says. I won't accept the testimony and evidence that come from Him." If God has recorded His promise in His Word and a man refuses to believe the Word he has to say, "I do not choose to accept the evidence that comes from a creditable witness." And Thomas had to discount these ten witnesses who bore testimony to what had happened.

Second, Thomas' doubt rested on ignorance. Obviously he didn't remember the Lord's statements that He would rise from the dead. He didn't know of the program that Christ had presented that He must go to Jerusalem, die, be buried and, on the third day, rise again from the dead. Because of his ignorance of the Word of God, Thomas said, "I don't believe that what you've told me could actually have happened." If he had retained Christ's statements in his mind, then the ten disciples' testimony would immediately have fallen into its proper place; and he would have said, "Yes, this is exactly what He said would happen." But because of his lack of knowledge of God's Word and Christ's pomise, he chose not to believe.

Thomas was also ignorant of God's power, for he knew

nothing of a resurrection from the dead. He had witnessed restorations before—that of the widow's son, of Jairus' daughter, of Lazarus—but all these were *restored* to die again. But now Jesus Christ had appeared in such a manner that it was evident His was no restoration. The disciples must have recognized the difference because of Christ's glorified body since the gospels record nothing about Christ suddenly materializing before them at any time before the resurrection. Evidently, in Thomas' mind, what they were describing could only be true of a resurrected, glorified body; and he was not familiar with the power of God which could raise the Son from the dead, glorify Him, and give Him a new, glorified body.

Many of our doubts arise from these very problems that Thomas faced. We have doubts because we do not know the Bible that gives us God's promises and outlines His program. Because of our ignorance of the Word of God, a thing seems unreasonable to us; and because we weigh it with our own minds and it seems unreasonable, we conclude that it cannot be true, and we choose to not believe. We also are ignorant of God's power. Evaluating everything in terms of what we would do in a particular situation, we conclude that God is just as we are, so He must do what we would do in similar circumstances. For example, an individual doubts his salvation and says, "I cannot believe that I am eternally saved." New believers often doubt their salvation.

A man came to my office several years ago, and I had the joy of pointing Him to Christ through the Word of God. Without my suggesting it, he dropped down beside his chair and poured out his heart to God, saying that he was accepting Jesus Christ as his Saviour. He walked out of my office radiantly happy. The next day he called me up and said, "I don't know whether I'm saved or not." Then he told me something he had done. In the light of God's Word, his action was wrong; and because he had sinned after he had accepted Christ, he couldn't conceive of the fact that he was still saved. So over the phone I read him a number of verses, and it satisfied him—until the next day. Phoning again, he said, "I just don't feel saved." Then he made this significant remark: "If I were God, and I had one who professed to be my son who did what I've done, I'd throw him out." In other words, "If I were God, this is the way I'd deal with him." He was trying to bring God down to his level in saying, "Since this is what I would do if I were God, God must do what I would do if I were God," and he was plagued with doubt. After that went on for about ten days, I said, "This isn't something we can settle over the phone. Let's get together." He came to my office again. When he walked in I said, "Well, how are things going?"

He said, "I just don't feel saved."

I said to him, "Are you married?" I knew he was.

He said, "Sure."

I said, "Do you always feel married?"

He started to make a remark and then realized that I was serious. He began to see what I was getting at, so he said, "You know, whether I feel married or not doesn't have anything to do with it. I am whether I feel it or not."

I said, "Did you ever realize that whether you feel saved or not has nothing to do with it?"

He said, "It doesn't?"

I said, "No. You've been plagued with doubts about your salvation because you're ignorant of God's Word and His power. The Word says, 'He that hath the Son hath life,' and the kind of life He has given you is everlasting life, but you didn't know that. You're plagued with doubts because you're ignorant of the power of God, for you feel that He is unable to keep that which has been committed unto Him against that day." We talked awhile, and that was the last time I ever had a phone call from him.

The man said, "If I were God, I would do so and so." And that was Thomas' attitude. Thomas said, "If I were God, this isn't the way I'd work." Because of his ignorance he brought God down to his level; and if God is no bigger than you are, no wonder you have doubts about your God.

Notice another thing about Thomas. Not only did he disbelieve in spite of the testimony, and not only did he doubt because of ignorance, but he avowed that he would trust only his own senses: "Except I shall see in his hands the print of the nails, and put my finger into the print of the nails, and thrust my hand into his side, I will not believe" (Jn 20:25). To Thomas the resurrection was irrational; he wanted rational evidence—evidence that he could touch, feel, see, measure, and determine for himself. Why? Because to him, his mind was the highest authority. This is the key to doubt. Faith trusts the word of the one making the promise or the declaration. Doubt says, "I will not trust anyone outside of myself. What I cannot subject to sensory tests, I will not accept." Thus, Thomas wanted to reduce everything to his rational level, and what he could satisfy himself about he would accept, and nothing more. That kind of approach makes anything beyond man's finite ability impossible.

Young people face this again and again in school where they sit under brilliant teachers. These instructors have studied until they have become specialists in many different areas. From their exalted position they tell their students a lot of things. They say the Bible can't possibly be the inspired Word of God without error from cover to cover. They say this earth evolved and was not the creation of God. They say the virgin birth is an utter impossibility. They say Christ's resurrection is a myth. They say it is impossible to be saved by trusting someone else. Why do they say these things? Not because they are dumb, but because they trust their own intellect and cannot receive anything beyond their own ability to demonstrate. They are just like Thomas. What they can see, handle, touch, taste, smell and weigh, they accept, and nothing more. That was Thomas' position. The knowledge of men fills our libraries, sends men to the moon, builds computers to do our work, and explores the mysteries of the human body and mind in the field of medicine. Overwhelmed by the ability of men to think and to discover and to plan and to build, we conclude that man's mind is limitless. But God says that the mind of man is not big enough to understand and know the things of God: "The natural man receiveth not the things of the Spirit of God: for they are foolishness unto him: neither can he know them, because they are spiritually discerned" (1 Co 2:14). When an unbeliever will accept only what he can understand or reason out, he is eliminating any possibility of understanding God and the things of God because they are outside his sphere. That is what Thomas did. He accepted what he could see and touch, and that was all. He would not accept the testimony of those who had seen Christ, had received His benediction and blessing, and had been given His power, the power of the Spirit.

An unbeliever will always be controlled by doubt. Don't expect him to believe. He can't do it. He must always be a skeptic ruled by doubts because he has no greater authority than his own mind. A believer may act and think just like an unbeliever. When a believer rejects a biblical testimony and the evidence in the lives of those who have trusted God, saying he will not accept anything unless he can see it for himself and think it through and, if it seems rational and reasonable, accept it, he is acting just like the unbeliever. Thomas was a saved man, there is no doubt about that. He had fellowshiped with the Lord for years. But he was acting just like an unbeliever, and his doubts came because he trusted his own mind instead of accepting the promise of God's Word.

Why do doubts come to God's children? I believe we have doubts for exactly the same reasons that Thomas did. We are ignorant of God's revelation. The light can dispel darkness if we let it shine, but where it doesn't shine, darkness will continue. Many of us are in doubt because of our ignorance of the Bible; we know so little of the power of God as it is revealed there. We conclude there are things that God simply could not do. Confronted by an almost hopeless situation, our mind tells us there is no way out. We begin to doubt God's love, His wisdom and His counsel or plan; and we don't turn to the Bible to read such promises as, "I can do all things through Christ which strengtheneth me" (Phil 4:13). Then doubts come in and take over because we have concluded that there is no help.

When we trust our minds and say that we will believe only what is reasonable to us, we have actually become practicing atheists. That is exactly what Thomas was when he refused to believe the disciples. Can a believer act like an atheist? Yes. In what way was Thomas any different from an atheist? The atheist looks into his test tube and says, "I'll accept what I can see and weigh and measure and prove mathematically"; and since he can't put God into his test tube, he says there is no God. It is not surprising that the Russian astronaut looked out of his window in space and said, "I didn't see God anywhere," and concluded that there was no God. He was trusting his own mind. Beware lest you become a practicing atheist by trusting your own intellect. Beware of reducing God to the level of your puny intellect like Thomas did by saying, "I will not believe."

But happily the story does not end there. For a whole

week Thomas continued in doubt and distress caused by his practical atheism. Then Christ appeared to the disciples again. I marvel at the Lord's restraint and thrill at His grace. We would not expect Him to demonstrate Himself to Thomas as He had done to the ten the week before, nor to materialize and to appear in Thomas' presence, nor to present His hands and His side so that Thomas could do what he said would be necessary for him to believe. But our Lord did all this. And here is the marvel of His grace: There was not a single word of reprimand. He didn't scold him; He didn't castigate him for his unbelief; and He didn't deliver a theological lecture on faith. The Lord simply presented Himself. When Thomas got one glimpse of the Lord, he fell before Him and said, "My Lord and my God."

Then Christ offered Thomas the privilege of doing what he said would be necessary to make him believe. He said he could put forth his finger and touch the nail holes and could thrust his hand into His side. But the Bible doesn't say Thomas did it. One glimpse of Christ and the doubts were gone because that look brought Thomas to the end of trusting in his own wisdom and caused him to acknowledge two things. First, he said, "My Lord." That meant "You are the one who has the right to be obeyed. You are the one who has the right to be followed." Then he said, "my God," or "You are the one to be believed; You are the one to be trusted." In saying "My Lord and my God," Thomas was giving expression to the same faith that he had rejected the week before when the ten disciples met him with the glad tidings, "We have seen the Lord."

What was it that changed Thomas from a practicing atheist to the one who looked into Christ's face and said, "My Lord, my God"? It was the personal, intimate presence of Jesus Christ. When doubt settles upon your mind—and doubt is always in the mind, not in the heart or the will, but in the

mind—it finds lodging first of all because you are trusting
your own wisdom and intellect, and are satisfied that you are
the highest authority to determine what is right and wrong,
what is to be believed and what is to be rejected. Martin
Luther once said that you can't keep the birds from flying
over your head, but you can keep them from nesting in your
hair. You can't keep doubt from coming into your mind, but
a doubt must be retained there or it will dissipate in the light
of the Word of God. If you insist on nourishing and retaining
your doubts they will grow. But if you bring them into
Christ's presence and expose them to the person of Christ,
then they will dissipate and God will reveal Himself through
His Son as the one to be trusted and believed. The light of
His countenance will cause the darkness of doubt to disap-
pear. When this mind is subjected to the mind of Christ
and to the truth of the Bible, we come to personal, intimate
fellowship with the Lord Jesus Christ. Doubts must vanish
as light dissipates darkness. May God deliver us from doubt
as we confess that He is our Lord and our God.

6

God's Answer to

THE PROBLEM OF IRRITABILITY

1 SAMUEL 16:14-23

Dr. Lewis Sperry Chafer said he was startled on one occasion when he was praying with Dr. Harry Ironside, an extremely gracious and kind man. Dr. Chafer was surprised to hear Dr. Ironside pray, "Lord, keep me from turning out to be a mean old man." It was evident from the kindliness and graciousness of Dr. Ironside's life that God heard and answered his prayer. Perhaps he had prayed thus because he was so conscious of the danger of becoming mean as the result of the complexities of life.

These modern days are days of great tensions and pressures. And just as a steam boiler has to have a safety valve, so we must have a safety valve to release the built-up pressures. Usually this valve takes the form of our becoming cross, mean, cranky, cantankerous, surly or irritable. But these responses to everyday pressures are not peculiar to our society. The Bible records the experience of a person who didn't evidence the tranquillity of the quiet, agrarian society in which he lived, rather his life showed the pressures of the complexities of modern life. First Samuel 16 tells of Saul, a man who in every sense of the word had become cross, surly, and irritable. Let us examine his character to see some of the causes of his irritability, and then consider the remedy for this irritability.

Saul had been crowned king after his subjects, the Israelites, had demanded a ruler. It was not God's choice to establish a monarchy, but He permitted Israel to have her own way; and Saul was set apart as king. Great responsibilities immediately descended upon Saul, and he found that the life of a king was not without its pressures and problems. He had difficulties in the international realm. He had to wage many battles. He had to drive enemies out of his borders. He had the responsibility of providing for his people. He had to face many economic problems because the people who had been set up on a family type of society were now being brought into an entirely new kind of society, of which he was the administrator. Untold religious problems plagued him because Saul was a man who in his early years set his heart after God but later turned away from God. He did not mind disobeying God when it pleased him. Setting himself up as a superior to God, his disobedience plagued the nation in the religious realm. All of these political, social, economic, and religious pressures descended upon him.

After Saul's disobedience the Spirit of the Lord departed from him and an evil spirit from the Lord troubled him (1 Sa 16:14). Saul had been a man controlled by the Spirit of God. God had worked through him and had brought blessing nationally, socially, politically, and economically to Israel. But because of his willful disobedience, because he set his face against God, the Spirit of the Lord departed from Saul; the Scripture says that an evil spirit from the Lord troubled him. This is not a demon, as some have supposed, because demons are not sent to do the will of God. They are not God's servants. Angelic beings which were created to be God's servants followed Lucifer in his rebellion and became servants of the wicked one. Since God does not dispatch demons to do His bidding, this was not a demon that came upon Saul to possess or control him. Rather, the evil spirit was an attitude, a disposition, a subtle character that came upon Saul because of his departure from the Lord. It might be referred to as an evil or a grieved conscience; and this disposition was the result of his progressive departure from the will of God.

In what sense then could it be said that this was an evil spirit from the Lord? This disposition was said to be from the Lord because it followed an inevitable law. If a man has walked with God and then turns away from Him, misery will inevitably settle upon him; and this law operated to such an extent in Saul's life that it could be said to be God's law that will operate when a man does what Saul did. Saul, who had known the joy of being an instrument in the hand of God, now had a wicked, evil, irritable disposition, which followed the inevitable progression of the law that a man who departs from God cannot experience the joy or the happiness of the Lord. Saul was characterized by giving way to malice, envy, bitterness, hatred, or general irritability.

After David had been summoned and had played his harp for the king, Saul was refreshed (16:23). Notice that phrase: Saul was refreshed. The word "refreshed" suggests that Saul's irritability, at least in measure or perhaps first of all, was the result of exhaustion, tiredness, and weariness, so that there was a very close connection between weariness and irritability. This weariness may have come from several causes or through a combination of them. There was reason to believe that Saul may have experienced physical exhaustion. After all, he had the sole responsibility of administering the government. He had led his troops in battle; he had fought to consolidate his borders and to preserve the geographical integrity of his people. Thus Saul appears, from the preceding chapters, to be a man who would be characterized by physical exhaustion.

Or, coupled with that may have been emotional exhaustion, for after all, in the verses that immediately precede,

Samuel, the prophet of God, was sent to Saul to anoint David as king. It was presumptuous to anoint a man king before the death of the present occupant of the throne. When word was brought to Saul that Samuel had anointed David as king, it could not have caused any other reaction than an emotional upheaval. He would have liked to vent his wrath on Samuel or David, but he could touch neither. The emotional response of hearing that Samuel had anointed another to take his place was certainly sufficient cause to produce this irritability.

Or his exhaustion may have been mental. Here he was a man alone coping with problems concerning the preservation of his kingdom, the maintenance of his borders, and the provision for his people which was his duty as king. The mental acumen required to discharge his office would stagger any man. He had no cabinet. He had no congress to make decisions and to implement plans. The responsibility was solely his. The situation was such that physically or emotionally or mentally, Saul could have known exhaustion. When David came, he was able to provide refreshment for the king; the refreshment referred to in verse 23 has to do with giving rest from the weariness. Whatever the cause of the weariness, David's music played a quieting part.

What did Saul need to solve his problem of irritability from weariness? The answer is obvious. He needed rest, and David provided rest through his music that could remove some of Saul's evil spirit or irritability. The great classical composers composed their music to produce emotional effects. They wanted to give peace, quietness, rest, relaxation, to stir love and the soothing emotions. What the modern composer wants to produce is anything but rest, and his music is designed to produce turmoil, and stress and strain within the individual. To prove this, observe that when your radio is tuned to some stations that blare out popular music and jazz

hour after hour, and you're trying to work, that music does
not give rest. It is music to be irritated by. You are piping
into your soul that which was designed to produce restlessness. As you listened you were producing a weariness within
you that in turn produced irritability. Thus, on many occasions when we become snappy and surly and cross and irritable it is because of physical or mental emotional exhaustion,
a great part of which we may be responsible for ourselves
because we have put ourselves under the influence of that
which will produce the very thing that we despise.

I had a very wise professor in college, a professor of Bible,
whose study was always open to us. As I advanced in my
studies and was taking a course theology, I would become
confused and distressed, and I would decide to visit that professor. Often it was late at night, but his study light was
burning; and I would knock on his door and ask if I could
talk to him for a few minutes. He would bring me into his
study and inquire about my problem. I would tell him. He
would listen to me and then say: "You're too tired to discuss
it tonight. I want you to go home and get a good night's
sleep, and then come back in the morning and talk with me
about it." He would never talk to me at night. His thought
was that when one is physically exhausted after a day's
studies and activities, he is in no condition to settle any of
these things. He knew that refreshment was necessary for
the relaxed attitude that was necessary to perceive spiritual
truths. Thus, first of all, Saul's irritability was the result of
exhaustion, and for this he needed rest.

Second, his irritability was the result of lost fellowship with
God. The first was in the realm of the physical. The second
was in the realm of the spiritual. Verse 14 says, "The Spirit
of the LORD departed from Saul." What led up to that? There
are two incidents in the book of 1 Samuel in which God
announced His displeasure with Saul. First, Saul had been

waiting for Samuel but Samuel did not respond to his summons (13:8). Finally Saul said "Bring hither a burnt offering to me, and peace offerings. And he offered the burnt offering" (v. 9). God had said that only a priest of the tribe of Levi could offer sacrifices to Him in an acceptable manner, and Saul was of the tribe of Benjamin. He therefore was ineligible to enter the priest's office and to officiate at a sacrifice, but he was so self-willed that he discounted God's word and presumed to enter the priest's office. When Samuel arrived he announced to Saul that he was to be removed from the throne because of his disobedience: "But now thy kingdom shall not continue: the LORD hath sought him a man after his own heart, and the LORD hath commanded him to be captain over his people, because thou hast not kept that which the LORD commanded thee" (v. 14).

Again, in chapter 15, God had given Saul a command to slay all of the enemy when he came up against them. But Saul preserved Agag, the king of the Amalekites, alive. Evidently Saul wanted to lead Agag in a great triumphal procession so that his countrymen might honor him. Thus he disobeyed God and spared Agag. Because of his disobedience in entering the priest's office and in sparing Agag, God said He would no longer use this disobedient, willful man as His servant; and the spirit of the Lord departed from Saul. This was a spiritual problem, and his irritability as it is manifest again and again after this point arose because Saul could not know the rest and the quietness of the Lord because he was out of fellowship with the God who had chosen him as His instrument.

Saul's irritability must be recognized as the product of the flesh, not the product of the Holy Spirit. That which characterizes the Holy Spirit is quietness, peaceableness, and rest; He will never produce that which is contrary to His own character in a child of God. Thus the Holy Spirit never pro-

duces irritability in the child of God. That is the product of
the flesh or the old nature. The child of God who walks in
disobedience or is controlled by the flesh will manifest the
irritability and the restlessness of his old father, the devil.
If the Spirit of God is in control, He will reproduce the quietness and peacefulness of Jesus Christ. Can you imagine
Christ being irritated and snapping somebody's head off? It
is ludicrous even to think about it. We need to recognize
that irritability such as Saul experienced is the product of the
flesh, a manifestation of the sin nature, and that it comes
when one is out of fellowship with the Lord Jesus Christ.

If this is the cause of irritability, the obvious solution is
found in 1 John 1:9, a passage to which we believers come
again and again. If we had been guilty of some gross sin, we
would run to 1 John 1:9, but seldom do we think of it in
relation to our irritability. We have set irritability outside
the realm of sin, failing to recognize that it is as much a
manifestation of the flesh as any of the catalog of sins in
Galatians 5. The only way that Saul could have gotten over
the irritability that was produced by his disobedience was to
confess that disobedience, offer sacrifice to God, and receive
forgiveness and restoration.

Contrast Saul with David on this point. Saul sinned, but
so did David. Society would probably say David's sin was
greater than Saul's. What was the difference between the
two men? In Psalm 32 David said that he was miserable until
he confessed his sin to God, and in Psalm 51:7, 12 he cried
out, "Purge me with hyssop, and I shall be clean: wash me,
and I shall be whiter than snow. Restore me unto the joy of
thy salvation." When David was in that period of his life, it
would have been amazing if he had not shown the same irritability that Saul had manifested toward him. Why? His
joy was gone for he was out of fellowship with God. But
David confessed his sin and acknowledged that it was sin,

and he was restored to a quietness and a peaceful disposition
so that God could use him. Therefore he wrote some of the
glorious psalms of praise while Saul went further and further
into his irritability until he was left alone because none could
tolerate him. The difference was David dealt with his problem, and Saul did not. On the one hand, irritability may be
caused by weariness, and for this there is need of rest. On
the other hand it may be produced by a lost fellowship and
for this there is no remedy but confession.

A third cause of irritability is found in 1 Samuel 16:22-23.
Saul's irritability was a sin against love. After he had been
counseled to find a musician who could give rest emotionally,
mentally, and physically, he sought out David, the sweet
singer of Israel. "And David came to Saul, and stood before
him: and he loved him greatly; and he became his armour-
bearer. And Saul sent to Jesse, saying, Let David, I pray
thee, stand before me; for he hath found favour in my sight"
(vv. 21-22). David loved Saul and became his armor-bearer,
and Saul loved David who ministered to his emotional and
physical and mental needs. The succeeding chapters show
David being hounded by Saul in manifestations of irritability
—a sin against love. When we think of love as the fruit of the
Spirit, instinctively we turn to 1 Corinthians 13: There the
apostle Paul comments on the product of love in the life of
the child of God. This is not natural love; it is a love that is
produced as God's Spirit reproduces Christ's love in the
believer. And after speaking of the preeminence of love, he
describes the product of love. "Charity suffereth long" (v.
4), or love endures patiently. That is the opposite of a short-
temper, a snappishness that characterizes irritability. Unlike
irritability, love is kind instead of being cutting. Love does
not envy; it is unselfish. It considers the good of the object
of love instead of a selfish consideration of itself. Love does
not become jealous or envious. Love does not lift itself up;

it does not put oneself in the preeminent position, which is one of the major problems in irritability.

Why do we become so upset at little things? Because these things have affected our plans. They changed what we purposed to do. They interrupted what we had in mind. When self becomes the center of one's life, then everything that goes contrary to self becomes upsetting and irritating. These little things become like thorns in the finger because self is put in the place of primary consideration. That is what Paul meant when he said love does not lift itself up or put itself in the place of preeminence so that everything is considered in the light of how it affects me. Love is not puffed up, does not think of itself as being in a superior position. We become irritated because we feel that we are the one due the consideration; and just as soon as somebody proposes something that seems to belittle or humiliate or deflate us a little bit, we begin to bristle. Love does not behave itself unseemly in a manner that leads one to question love. But when we become so surly and backbiting and caustic in speech, we certainly give others the right to question our affection. "Love seeketh not her own"; she does not put herself in the center position, is not easily stirred up to hostility, does not become suspicious.

Paul is showing the pattern of love that the Holy Spirit uses and is contrasting that to irritability, the product of the flesh. The Spirit reproduces the loveliness of Christ, and the flesh reproduces the heinous character of Satan in the child of God. Saul in his irritability was sinning against David's love for him and his love for David. Irritability toward the brethren is the product of the flesh, the product of the old sin nature that prevents the Spirit from reproducing Jesus Christ in us; we reproduce our father the devil in our daily actions and speech and tongue. Saul is one of the most tragic characters in all the Word of God, a man who started with a

noble beginning but became a dismal failure. In every sense
of the word he became a mean old man.

That is the natural progression of life unless the Spirit of
God controls an individual. Saul needed rest and refreshment.
Perhaps we need more physical rest. Saul needed to keep
short accounts with God and make certain that his irritable-
ness was not because he was out of fellowship. And when we
realize that we are in just such a position, we need to go
aside quietly and to take stock to see whether the flesh has
dominated and there is something we need God to deal with
in the light of 1 John 1:9. We must recognize that God has
commanded us to love one another, and a failure to obey that
command is to sin against love. Irritability is a prevalent
problem, but it is a problem about which the Word of God
has very practical suggestions. Examine Saul's life again to
see if you can see his traits reproduced in you.. Recognize
that this may be a physical problem, or it may be a spiritual
problem, but it certainly is a sin against love and must be
dealt with as any other sin. May God the Holy Spirit reproduce the love of Christ in us so that we shall show His
love to all men.

7

God's Answer to
THE PROBLEM OF
DISCOURAGEMENT

1 KINGS 19:9-18

> Breathes there a man with soul so dead,
> That never to himself has said, "I'm beat!"

That which seems to be common experience of men is reflected many times over in the Word of God, for many of us are subject to the discouragement that produces despair. No commanding officer would want to lead his men into the battle unless he were assured that they had a heart for the fight, for if they had lost the heart to fight they have already lost the battle. Discouragement is the loss of courage. When an English word begins with the prefix *dis*, it simply means that the person being described has lost whatever the rest of the word suggests. The man who is discouraged has lost courage, has lost heart, has lost the will to fight; and the discouraged man is a defeated man.

When Satan wants to gain victory over a man and keep him from fighting the good fight of faith, he does not have to throw an unconquerable foe against that individual. All he has to do is change the person's attitude toward victory, for when that man is convinced that victory is no longer possible, he is already defeated. Satan does not enjoy bringing God's children into an arena for a contest for supremacy. He delights in keeping the child of God from ever entering the arena by discouraging him before he begins. Day by day we have to fight the battle of discouragement and faintheartedness in the fight of faith. Discouragement is principally self-occupation. A man is discouraged because he has turned his eyes inward upon himself, and he evaluates all things in terms of himself. He sees every situation in its effect upon him personally and, being totally occupied with himself, he is easily discouraged because he knows he is inadequate for any situation. While it is true that the believer can do all things through Christ who strengthens him, it is also true that by himself the child of God can do nothing; and as soon as he is no longer occupied with Jesus Christ but becomes occupied with himself, he is ready prey to discouragement.

Three of God's saints were totally discouraged and completely defeated to the point that they thought the only solution to their discouragement was physical death. They were so low in their defeat and discouragement that they cried out to God that He would take their lives. But thanks be to God, physical death is not the solution to discouragement.

The first of these saints was Moses, and the record of his discouragement is in Numbers 11. Presumably Moses would have been above this problem and not subject to this particular attack of Satan. He had seen the hand of God work on his behalf, bringing him and those for whom he was responsible from victory to victory. He had been specially trained by God as a leader and deliverer of people through his forty years with God in the backside of the desert. God brought Moses back into Egypt after his exile and entrusted such authority to him as man had never before exercised; and Moses in the presence of pharaoh and the Egyptians wrought signs and miracles to confirm him as a leader of God's people and to authenticate the God whom he served. Moses had seen God deliver Israel out of Egypt by blood. He had seen God's bared right arm as He took them on dry land through the Red Sea and brought them as free men out of Egypt. Moses had been on the mount with God, had communed with God face to face, and had received the greatest revelation of God's holiness that any man had received since the fall. We might presume that a man who had had these experiences would forever be delivered from discouragement and the despair that discouragement brings, but Moses became totally defeated, totally discouraged—so much that he cried out, "I am not able to bear all this people alone, because it is too heavy for me. And if thou deal thus with me, kill me, I pray thee, out of hand, if I have found favour in thy sight; and let me not see my wretchedness" (Num 11:14-15). Moses was so wretched that he preferred to die than continue in the surrounding circumstances, and he felt his death would be a favor from the hand of God. What produced such discouragement in Moses' life? The mixed multitudes that had come with the children of Israel out of Egypt had not given up their appetite for the foods of Egypt. When they had to depend upon God and live on the bread of heaven, they found that they had no taste for it because a heavenly appetite was necessary to enjoy feeding on the bread of heaven, and they didn't have that appetite. They lusted for the cucumbers and melons and leeks and onions and garlic and the fish of the land of Egypt. They had a problem with the menu out there because they ate manna morning, noon, and night; and everytime they put the manna in their mouths they longed for a little garlic to go along with it so that it would taste like home. The people in their rebellion cried out against the Lord and against Moses: "Then Moses heard the people weep throughout their families, every man in the door of his tent: and the anger of the LORD was kindled greatly; Moses also was displeased" (v.

10). As Moses poured out his heart to God, notice what a prominent place his ownself held in Moses' thinking, He saw the whole multitude lusting for the foods of Egypt; and, instead of thinking of what it revealed about them or how that lust affected them, he could only think of how their lust affected him. So he said to God, "Wherefore hast thou afflicted thy servant?" (v. 11). Why are you doing this to me?"

> Wherefore have I not found favour in thy sight, thou thou layest the burden of all this people upon me? Have I conceived all this people? Have I begotten them, that thou shouldest say unto me, Carry them in thy bosom, as a nursing father bearest the sucking child, unto the land which thou swarest unto their fathers? Whence should I have flesh to give unto all this people? For they weep unto me, saying, Give us flesh, that we may eat. I am not able to bear all this people alone, because it is too heavy for me (11:11-14).

While God had placed the responsibility of leadership upon Moses, He had not surrendered His personal care over Israel. He had promised that He would provide for Israel. He would protect His people on their wilderness journey. Moses' problem came when he assumed and took upon himself the responsibility that belonged to God and which God had not placed upon him. It was God's responsibility to give them food to eat, but Moses took it as his responsibility. God had said that He would bear them as a father bears his children out of Egypt and bring them into the land. But Moses assumed he had to do it. Becoming totally occupied with himself, he saw the murmuring and every complaint as a personal attack. When he became occupied with himself and became the center of his interests and attention, Moses broke under the load and gave way to complete discouragement.

Furthermore, not only did Moses assume a responsibility

which was God's, but he saw only the failure of the people. He was focusing his attention upon their weakness. Concentrating on their stumbling, their rebellion, and their lack of faith, he became so occupied with the failures of those who professed to be pilgrims on their way to the land of promise that he could not see God's faithfulness. Viewing everything in relationship to himself, he thought that because the people had failed, he had failed, and because they had complained, that he was responsible to meet their cry. And as he listened to them and turned a deaf ear to God's promise and voice, he assumed the complaint of the people was against him, Moses became so discouraged that he cried out, "Do me a favor and kill me so that I don't have to continue in my misery any longer."

But it was here that God intervened and sought to direct Moses' eyes away from himself and back to the Lord. God did several things. First, He gave Moses seventy men of the elders of Israel to help bear his responsibility. When the children of Israel first came out of Egypt, they were going through a trackless desert. They did not know the way that they were to take, and Moses procured his father-in-law as a guide. A resident of that area of the country, he became eyes for Moses and for the children of Israel. As his father-in-law watched Moses operate, he saw that Moses was being called upon to personally settle every litigation that arose among the children of Israel. His father-in-law advised him to select seventy men, elders in the congregation, and give them some administrative authority so that they could handle the small, tedious details and Moses could take care of the big things. And the saying pleased Moses and he appointed seventy. God recognized the institution of the seventy men appointed by Moses but He went a step further. He said He would "come down and talk with thee there: and I will take of the spirit which is upon thee, and will put it upon them; and they shall bear the burden of the people with thee, that thou bear it not thyself alone" (11:17). God never placed the responsibility upon Moses. It was God's responsibility and, by empowering these seventy men, He was giving Moses a visible demonstration that He was not asking him, and never had asked him, to assume the responsibility for the whole administration himself. The appointment of these seventy men was designed to be a reminder to Moses that the responsibility was God's, that He would be faithful to it. God appointed these seventy on whom Moses would call so that Moses would not give way to discouragement because he had assumed God's responsibility which was too big for him.

Notice a second thing as God moves to meet Moses' need. When the people cried, "Who shall give us flesh to eat?" (v. 18a). Moses promised, "The LORD will give you flesh" (v. 18b). God did that which Moses had promised the people He would do. God sent them flesh to eat. Now it is true that in sending the flesh, the flesh became a judgment from God; but observe that when Moses promised them flesh to eat, God performed a miracle to provide it. Moses was willing to let God assume the responsibility and simply announce to the people what God would do. Moses turned the problem over to God, and God assumed the responsibility. He gave the people that which they desired and Moses was delivered from the despondency of discouragement and defeat.

In this instance Moses' experience is a very vital lesson for us because much discouragement which we face and which overthrows us comes because we assume a responsibility or an obligation which God has never placed upon us. We can see how readily, for instance, this temptation will meet a missionary of the cross. They go to a strange land to meet a strange people. Perhaps they feel responsible for a tribe of tens of thousands of people who have no written language, nothing of the Word of God, no knowledge of Jesus Christ;

and they look at the multitudes that are to be reached by the gospel. If they concentrate upon the enormity of the task they will go down in defeat and discouragement because they are not capable of discharging that responsibility. God sent them there to be faithful as a witness to Himself. The work of converting men is God's work, not theirs. If they can rightly relate to God's program, then they can be delivered from the despair of discouragement; but if they assume an obligation that is not theirs, then they are hopelessly inadequate and will certainly be defeated by discouragement.

Moses' failure came because he did not leave God's responsibility in his hands and assume only that which God had entrusted to him. Unless we can discern between what is our responsibility and what is God's, then we like Moses will assume that which we cannot fulfill and will go down in discouragement and defeat. God had promised to provide and it was Moses' responsibility to let God fulfill His promise. When he tried to fulfill God's promise for God, he could not do it, and discouragement was certainly the result of his lack of trust and faith. Moses' experience teaches us that we must distinguish between that which is our responsibility and that which is God's. Then we must assume that which is ours and leave with God that which is His, trusting Him to do in and through us that which He has promised.

Another of God's saints gave way to discouragement to the point that he pleaded with God to take him away by death. Elijah had been raised up by God to be a prophet in the midst of apostasy and unbelief. It seemed as though the nation to a man had gone after the heathen gods introduced by Ahab's attractive queen. The daughter of a foreign king, she had brought her father's idols with her when she came into Israel, and corrupted the nation by leading them away from God to her idols. Elijah stood out alone against the corruption of the court, against the wickedness of king and the queen, and against the idolatry that had been introduced in the nation. Because of his opposition, Jezebel sent a messenger to him with the announcement that she was going to have his head. She would not permit him to preach against her within the confines of her kingdom, and she gave him twenty-four hours to live. "So let the gods do to me, and more also, if I make not thy life as the life of one of them by to morrow about this time" (1 Ki 19:2). And Elijah fled. "He himself went a day's journey into the wilderness, and came and sat down under a juniper tree: and he requested for himself that he might die; and said, It is enough; now O LORD, take away my life; for I am not better than my fathers" (19:4). Evidently he had gone all day long without any food or water to sustain him. So desperate was his plight he could think only of getting beyond the long arm of Jezebel; and when he was physically weakened, he became spiritually weakened and discouragement swept over him. God awoke him through an angel who said to him, "Arise and eat."

In meeting this problem of Elijah's discouragement, notice that God didn't deal with the spiritual problem first. He dealt with the physical problem. This leads us to the very important observation that frequently these problems which seem to be in the spiritual realm are directly traceable to weakness in the physical realm. Had this been early morning when he could still be sustained by a good solid meal that he had the night before, things might have looked much different to him. But after he was physically depleted through fleeing throughout the day, along with his physical tiredness and weakness there came this spiritual weakness, and disappointment swept over his soul. The angel didn't say, "Elijah, you're discouraged. Get down on your knees and pray." The angel said, "Get up and eat. When you have eaten then you will be prepared to deal with this problem." "And he looked, and, behold, there was a cake baken on the coals, and a cruse of water at his head. And he did eat and drink, and laid him down again" (19:6). Then the angel spoke a second time and said, "Arise and eat." He didn't have enough that first time. The sustenance was such that Elijah was able to live forty days in the wilderness on the strength of that meat (v. 8). This was God's divine provision for him. For forty days he went in the strength of that divine provision until once again he was physically exhausted. Then Elijah found himself in a cave where he took up lodging, hidden away from Jezebel, and the threat of death that hung over him. But the word of the Lord came to him and said, "What doest thou here, Elijah?" Again Elijah was thinking of himself. Notice how he had become the center of attention in his own mind! Discouragement is self-occupation and, occupied with himself, physical strength ebbed away, and defeat and discouragement gripped him. "I have been very jealous for the LORD God of hosts: for the children of Israel have forsaken thy covenant, thrown down thine altars, and slain thy prophets with the sword; and I, even I only, am left; and they seek my life, to take it away" (v. 10). Here was a man, like Moses, totally discouraged and defeated and, crushed because of the death sentence of Jezebel, who concluded that it would be better for him to die at God's hand than to have to keep running from this wicked woman who shared Ahab's throne.

God moved to meet the problem of discouragement. The first thing that He said to Elijah was that he must get busy in the work that God had for him to do (v. 15). He said that he was to anoint Hazael to be king over Syria, and Jehu was to be anointed king over Israel, and Elisha was to be anointed to be prophet in Elijah's place. Now this meant a good deal of traveling. Elijah would have to go up to Syria on the north to Damascus; he would have to seek out Jehu in Israel in the northern kingdom, and then he would have to seek out Elisha

and anoint him. In other words, there was work to be done,
there was a ministry to be performed, and this was no time
for Elijah to be hiding in a cave feeling sorry for himself,
occupied with himself, and commiserating with himself that
he was the only one left in the whole nation that had not gone
into apostasy. In order for Elijah to get over this disappointment and this defeat, he had to get busy with the work that
God had entrusted to him. A man who is occupied with God
and occupied for God cannot at the same time very well be
occupied with himself. We live with ourselves so much it is
easy for us to become self-occupied; and unless we are occupied with God, our minds will drift unconsciously to ourselves and our needs, problems, defeats and discouragements,
and we fall in the fray. So the first thing that God said to
Elijah was that there was work to be done and He wanted
him to be doing it.

The second thing that God said to Elijah was: "I have left
me seven thousand in Israel, all the knees which have not
bowed unto Baal, and every mouth which hath not kissed
him" (v. 18). Elijah was discouraged because he stood alone
for God. He felt he was the only one who had a heart for
God. Perhaps these 7,000 who had not bowed the knee to
Baal may have been some of the fruits of Elijah's ministry.
Some who had heard him denounce the idolatry introduced
by Jezebel may have been toying with the idea of giving up
their obedience to Jehovah and going after this strange god
who didn't make such stringent demands upon them. They
may have been prevented from that deviation from God's
revealed truth by the prophet's faithful proclamation. Elijah
didn't know anything about it; he didn't know the effects of
his ministry. He didn't know how God used his witness and
how God had preserved them. But God told the prophet
that there were 7,000 who had not bowed the knee to Baal so

that Elijah could see a little of the fruits of his ministry and be encouraged in the midst of discouragement.

Elijah's experience holds a very practical lesson for us. God puts a ministry before us, but many times physical weakness or infirmity turns our eyes upon ourselves and away from God and the ministry entrusted to us, and we become so totally occupied with ourselves that the work is left undone. Discouragement takes over. That's where Elijah was. There was work to be done, but he was hiding in a cave. Physical weakness certainly contributed to his discouragement, but God took care of that. Still he was discouraged. So God drew back the curtain and let this man of God see a little bit of the fruits of his labor to encourage him to complete the task entrusted to him.

Yet a third man cried out that God would take his life. The prophet Jonah had a good deal to be discouraged about. God had sent him to pronounce judgment upon Nineveh, the capital of the Assyrian Empire. The Assyrians were the great threat to Israel's national existence, and Jonah knew that unless God destroyed Nineveh, they would move into Israel and swallow her up. Jonah in his natural thinking had decided that the best way to solve the situation was to withhold the message of life from Nineveh, let them move against the people of Israel, and then let God swat them down like flies and exterminate them. Thus, the great oppressor of Israel would be taken away. But God had His way of getting the prophet in the right place at the right time, and he went through the experience with a great fish to get where God wanted him to be. Jonah moved through the city of Nineveh, crying as he went, "Forty days and this city shall be destroyed by Almighty God!" A city the size of Dallas turned to God, cast themselves upon His mercy, and pleaded for forgiveness; and God in His infinite grace delivered that Gentile city from divine judgment.

Jonah was perplexed. Can you imagine a man being so used of God to turn multitudes to God who would become discouraged by his success? That is exactly what happened, for Jonah went up to the east side of the city and made a booth where he might sit in the shade till he could see what would happen to the city if perchance God would change His mind and destroy it (chap. 4). As Jonah was sitting there under the hot sun, God caused a gourd to grow up over that empty framework that gave no shade; the gourd vine protected Jonah from the sun, and he was glad because of it. The next morning Jonah went out and found that a worm had gnawed off the vine, and the gourd was dead; so the vine no longer protected Jonah from the sun. The sun arose and God sent a vehement east wind that burned and blistered the prophet. But what was happening to his skin wasn't as bad as what was happening to him inside. He "fainted, and wished in himself to die, and said, It is better for me to die than to live" (4:8). God tried to teach a lesson to this prophet who suddenly had become so occupied with himself and with his reputation as a prophet that he could not bless God who had brought deliverance to such a multitude of Gentiles. God said in effect, "Jonah, you didn't spend anything on that gourd. It came up because I planted it, but you rejoiced in it because it brought benefit to you. Can't you see, Jonah, that these Gentiles will bring honor and glory to Me, and I will be glorified by the salvation of this whole city? And Jonah, why do you sit there discouraged and defeated? Is it because you are afraid to go back home, for fear your own people will despise you for going to the Gentiles?" Jonah would have had no problem if the Gentiles had rejected his message. He would have had no problem if he had pronounced the judgment and it had fallen, because then all of his countrymen would have welcomed him home with opened arms, saying that the judgment was the greatest sign of his prophetic gift and office that they had ever seen. But when God blessed Gentiles, Jonah sat there feeling concerned for himself, his reputation, and how he was going to face his people again. And his solution to the problem was that God should strike him dead.

What contributed to Jonah's discouragement? It was a common problem that we face. We cannot understand God's workings. His methods of dealing with us are often so far beyond us that we cannot fathom them; therefore, we think that God can't fathom them either, and we conclude that He doesn't know what He is doing. That is why multitudes think that they are not in the hands of God. They feel they are in the hands of fate and that fate is carrying them along blindly with no plan, purpose, aim nor goal. All things are not moving in God's infinite wisdom, they say. Things just happen. That is why even many Christians when they are taking leave of one another say, "Good luck!" That means that there isn't a God who is controlling things. Luck is in control. That was the mind of Jonah. He could not understand God's workings because he was ignorant of God's revealed word. God had revealed from the time that He had called Abraham and blessed Israel that He was going to bless Gentiles. God had said to Abraham, the father of Israel, "In thee and in thy seed shall all the families of the earth be blessed" (Gen 28:14). Jonah was obviously ignorant of God's purpose to bring the blessing of salvation to all men, to provide a Saviour who would bring them to God. Because Jonah was ignorant of God's purpose and plan, he was ignorant of His program. He could not see God's hand moving in the circumstance in which he was involved and, leaving God out of the picture, all he had to put into that vacuum was himself. He became so occupied with himself that God was left out of the picture.

So many times when the circumstances of life threaten to engulf us and we become occupied with what we are going through, we forget that we are in the hand of Christ. And Christ is in the hand of God, so we are doubly secure and doubly safe. We forget that God has a purpose for His child that involves every single detail in His child's life. We forget that He is conforming us to Jesus Christ and has selected just the things to bring in our experience to do that perfecting in order that Christ's image might be revealed in us. Because we forget God's purpose, power, and program, we become occupied with the method He is using to accomplish His purpose, and we become defeated and discouraged and give way to despair. Then we say, "I wish the Lord would come." That is another way of saying, "It's just too much for me. Lord, let me die."

When Satan succeeds in directing our attention to ourselves, he has us focusing on that which is incapable of performing the ministries and responsibilities entrusted to us. He has us paying attention to one who is insufficient for the strain and test, one who is ignorant of God's purpose and plan. No wonder we succumb to discouragement and lose heart. We lay aside the armor and lay down the sword, and look for some cave to hide in. When we focus our attention upon Christ and obey the injunction of the apostles, "looking unto Jesus the author and finisher of our faith," and "run with patience the race that is set before us" (Heb 12:1b-2a), we can run assuredly and triumphantly without the plague of discouragement because we know that we are in God's hands, and that He will fulfill His purpose, and provide, direct, and accomplish His perfect will in and through us. If you feel companionship with Moses or Elijah or Jonah and have looked for a wilderness or a cave in which to hide, look away from yourself and look to the Lord Jesus Christ; He is the one who removes faintness from the heart and gives valor for the battle.

8

God's Answer to

THE PROBLEM OF MONOTONY

EZEKIEL 4:1-8

All of us at one time or another delight to pick up a travel magazine or the *National Geographic* to leaf through it and see those exciting faraway places. We have wished that we suddenly could be transported out of the dull monotony of the routine in which we find ourselves to these exotic lands where life would be so different. But the lot of most of us is to move not in these exciting, distant climes, but in the same circle day after day after day where life becomes routine. Because of the monotony, we strain to break the circle and get out into some new kind of existence. We dream of what it would be like to be a free-lance photographer and go from one place to another in the pursuit of excitement, or an international traveler who goes from country to country, or perhaps a news reporter who visits Paris and then London and then Rome, stopping off at a few good restaurants en route.

However, we must face the monotony of life as it really is. To many it seems as though we're caught up in the routine of a life that just isn't worth living. The housewife is especially subject to this feeling, for she bids farewell to her husband in the morning and thinks of the excitement to which he is going in the business world and all of the joy that it holds and the thrill of competition. Then she turns to the stack of dishes and the dusting and the mending and the cooking and the cleaning to keep the household going. The Lord has given me one of the most exciting works that a man could possibly have—ministering the gospel of Jesus Christ as a pastor and a teacher. Certainly no two days are ever quite the same, nor are any two hours in any day quite alike; and yet, God did give me enough experience, particularly in my student days, to know something of the monotony of a dull work routine. I have known the monotony of sitting at a typewriter cutting mimeograph stencils twelve hours a day, six days a week, for fifty dollars a month. I hate the smell of stencils to this day! I have stood on my feet all day long to feed rods into a threading machine—work that a trained monkey could do. Monotonous? Yes, but I have thanked God that I have had these experiences because I can appreciate what people go through living this monotonous kind of existence, where life becomes a drudgery and it seems that the only thing they have to look forward to is a two-week vacation before they return to the monotony. Does God have an answer to such an existence? When things have lost their glamour and are dull and routine, does He have any solution?

The prophet Ezekiel put in about as monotonous a period of time as a man could possibly endure. He did it in the will of God. He did it in obedience to God's command, and God gave him victories in doing it. It was necessary for God to chasten the nation Israel because of their apostasy, idolatry, unbelief, and lawlessness; and God brought Nebuchadnezzar from Babylon into the land of Judah and delivered Jerusalem into his hand. Nebuchadnezzar came on three different occasions. The first time he took away a handful of choice young men whom he trained to administer the affairs of the deportees in Babylon. Daniel was among that group—a brilliant young man prepared for a position of responsibility. Then in the second deportation, Nebuchadnezzar carried away a great many of the people, and evidently Ezekiel was

among that group. Not until a few years later did he come
a third time and completely destroy Jerusalem.

When Ezekiel was carried away into Babylon, he was set
apart by God to be His spokesman. "The word of the LORD
came expressly unto Ezekiel the priest . . ." (1:3). God
spoke to Ezekiel, called him to a ministry, and began preparing him for a ministry to those deportees. They were cut off
from Jerusalem and their homeland, from all familiar sur-
roundings. The nation had lost its independence and was in
subjection to a Gentile overlord. All their national hopes
seemed dashed and lost, and yet God had a program for
them. He purposed in His own time to restore them to the
land, to send them their Messiah, their King who would reign
over them in righteousness and justice and would institute
peace on the earth. So God raised up Ezekiel in order to
bring a message to this people. In their despair, discouragement and despondency, Ezekiel was to bring first of all a
note of judgment to explain why God had overthrown Jerusalem, and also, a note of comfort—what God would do for
them in a coming day. The prophet was commissioned:

> And he said unto me, Son of man, go, get thee unto the
> house of Israel, and speak with my words unto them. For
> thou art not sent to a people of a strange speech and of an
> hard language, but to the house of Israel; not to many peo-
> ple of a strange speech and of an hard language, whose
> words thou canst not understand. Surely, had I sent thee to
> them, they would have hearkened unto thee. But the house
> of Israel will not hearken unto thee; for they will not
> hearken unto me: for all the house of Israel are impudent
> and hardhearted. Moreover he said unto me, Son of man,
> all my words that I shall speak unto thee receive in thine
> heart, and hear with thine ears. And go, get thee to them
> of the captivity, unto the children of thy people, and speak
> unto them. Then the spirit entered into me, and set me

upon my feet, and spake with me, and said unto me, Go, shut thyself within thine house (3:4-7, 10-11, 24).

God said to the prophet, "Go and speak"; but when the prophet said, "Yes, Lord, I'm willing to speak," God said, "I want you to go home and shut the door and stay there. Hide yourself away."

I don't know what went through Ezekiel's mind when God called him. Perhaps he had thought he would be like Isaiah and minister in the king's court, or be elevated to a position of responsibility and eat at the king's table, be clothed with the king's raiments, enjoy a life of ease, and be honored and respected throughout the world. Or perhaps he thought he might be like Daniel. Daniel was put in a place of responsibility and was given administrative authority; and he was in charge of the nation's affairs as a prime minister. Perhaps Ezekiel thought God was preparing him to become a prime minister in Babylon. He may have thought of Jonah, for God called Jonah and then gave him a ticket and sent him on a tour to a foreign nation; and Ezekiel may have thought that he would travel too and see some of these faraway places. It must have been exciting to think of where God might send him. But after God called him and encouraged him, He said, "I want you to go home and close your door and stay there." Life suddenly became commonplace. It became routine. I venture to say that it became very monotonous.

But one day God broke that monotony by imposing an even worse monotony upon the prophet—perhaps as monotonous an existence as you can imagine (4:1-8). The prophet must have rejoiced when God loosed the latch of his home and sent him out. God asked Ezekiel to convey his message in a unique and a singular way. No prophet who preceded Ezekiel had conveyed his message in just this manner. God sent him out into the market place, into the highways and byways where multitudes of people were passing by, and told Ezekiel to

make a spectacle of himself for God's sake. God had told
the prophet that they would not hearken unto God and they
would not hearken unto him (3:7). If the prophet had stood
up and preached, not one of those captives would have paid
the least bit of attention. So God devised a new method of
visual education to get His point across. "Don't waste your
breath preaching to them," He said. "They won't listen. But
you can convey a message to them." God said, "This shall be
a sign to the house of Israel" (4:3). The prophet was to
select a large enough tile on which he could trace the outline of the city of Jerusalem. In those days the people made
square, flat tiles for roofing their houses. On this tile Ezekiel
traced the outline of Jerusalem, and every one of those Jewish deportees who looked at what was on that tile immediately recognized it.

If you see an artist with an easel, you crane your neck to
see what he is painting. When they asked, "What are you
doing?" Ezekiel didn't answer a word. It was no use explaining for they couldn't understand because of their spiritual
blindness. Putting that tile with the city of Jerusalem drawn
on it down on the ground, he began to play toy soldiers. It
appeared as though Ezekiel were completely out of his mind
because he built a trench around the city on the tile and he
put up mounds of dirt around it. Then he placed an army
around the tile, "and lay siege against it, and build a fort
against it, and cast a mount against it; set the camp also
against it, and set battering rams against it round about"
(4:2). That was the method Nebuchadnezzar used to defeat
a city. He would equip his soldiers with baskets, which they
loaded with dirt. Then they would dump the dirt against a
city wall. The pile of dirt got higher and higher until the
army could mount the wall and go over it without tearing it
down. Thus, Ezekiel's actions pictured the siege of the city.
Next, God told Ezekiel to take an iron pan and put it "be-

tween thee and the city: and set thy face against it, and it shall be besieged, and thou shalt lay siege against it" (v. 3). Evidently the frying pan had the same significance then as it does now when you say "out of the frying pan into the fire." It was the picture of judgment, of destruction, of a fierce siege that would destroy or consume all that was in it, After the prophet had drawn the city and put all of his soldiers in order and set up the frying pan as a sign of judgment, then God told him to lie down on his left side where God would bind the prophet. "I will lay bands upon thee, and thou shalt not turn thee from one side to another, till thou hast ended the days of thy siege" (v. 8). For 390 days the prophet was to lie bound in that unmovable position to be a sign to Israel. After the 390 days had expired, God instructed him to turn over, and to lie on his other side for 40 more days.

For well over a year the prophet did nothing except lie there in his bound position. The people passed him by. They looked at him. No word was spoken. He ate the coarsest of food. In fact, the food that he ate was to be baked over a fire of dung, thus it was defiled and unclean. For 430 days he just lay there. This was a monotonous existence. The number 430 was significant to an Israelite because it was the duration of the exile in Egypt. Many feel that these 430 days were to remind them of chastening because they were out of God's will. Others feel the number refers to the period of time that Israel had abandoned God and had turned from His law and walked in apostasy under her kings. There are a number of different explanations, but the point is very clear: this 430-day period signifies a time of judgment because of iniquity.

There are many indications as to what sustained the prophet during this difficult period of his ministry. First, he was acting in perfect obedience to God's will. If he had been asked, "Ezekiel, why are you here?" there could have been

only one answer: "Because God told me to be here." God
had called him. God had commissioned him. Then God gave
him the message, and even though the message was delivered
in the most unique way that a prophet had ever delivered his
message, yet he was there by divine appointment. It never
entered Ezekiel's mind, as far as the record goes, to question
God's wisdom or counsel. And the assurance that this was
God's will for him sustained the prophet during these 430
days when he was bound and immobilized. The commonplace was glorified when it was endured in the will of God,
and the prophet could glory in preaching by that experience
as much as the prophet Isaiah could glory when he proclaimed chapter 53 faithfully to the nation Israel. It wasn't
the form in which the message was delivered that was important. It was the fact that it was delivered in complete obedience to God's will. That which will sustain any man, no
matter how routine his day may be, is the assurance and
knowledge that he is in the will of God and that he is acting
in obedience to God's will.

This applies not just to one who may have been called to
go to the mission field or to teach or preach the Word of God
from a pulpit. It applies to the young person who goes to
school day after day after day and finds it very monotonous.
It applies to the man who goes to the business office and has
never risen above the routine in his business life, who finds
himself enmeshed in a system from which there is no relief,
and he is oppressed by it. It applies to the housewife who
has to go through the menial tasks of the day that take so
little brainpower to perform. If what you are doing is God's
will for you, then you can know His joy in obedience as much
as did Ezekiel, Isaiah, or Daniel.

The New Testament emphasizes this principle again and
again. Peter deals with this question of submission: "Submit
yourselves to every ordinance of man for the Lord's sake"

(1 Pe 2:13). Notice that he is dealing here with the political realm, the realm of state, the realm of law; and he enjoins the child of God to be in perfect obedience to those who are in authority, "whether it be to the king, as supreme; or unto governors, as unto them that are sent by him for the punishment of evildoers, and for the praise of them that do well" (vv. 13-14). What is their attitude in submitting to the government? They are to do it for the Lord's sake (v. 13), and again, "For so is the will of God" (v. 15). Do you see the connection between obedience to God and daily life? The apostle says that we are to give the same obedience in this daily routine that we would give to God personally. When he moves to another realm, the same principle obtains: "Be subject to your masters [your employers] with all fear; not only to the good and gentle [those who are easy to get along with] but also to the froward [the cantankerous, the ornery]. For this is thankworthy if a man for conscience toward God endure grief" (vv. 18-19). What is it that is to produce the obedience of employee to employer? Conscience toward God. We're to give the employer the same obedience that we would give to God. Why? Because that is God's will for us. God didn't ask Ezekiel, "How would you like to be tied up for 430 days and be made a spectacle out there in the highway?" No, God said to Ezekiel, "Go," and he went. As he was going, God revealed the first thing that He wanted him to do, and Ezekiel did it without question and without reservation. Why? Because it was God's will. The knowledge that this was God's will sustained him through the monotony of what is perhaps one of the longest sermons ever preached—430 days.

If the child of God does not know he is in the will of God in this daily round of activities, then he had better get out of it. He had better find out what God's will is. But if one goes to the daily routine with the confidence that this is God's

will for him and then he begins to rebel against what God
appoints for him to do in that day, he is rebelling not only
against the monotony of the job, he is rebelling against God.
So much of what he would classify as justifiable complaint
against monotony is really undisguised rebellion against God.
Why should a child of God have anything but joy in doing
God's will? And if His will becomes monotonous, then we
had better examine ourselves to see first if we're in His will
and if our attitude toward His will is the correct attitude.
Certain things about my work as a teacher could be considered very monotonous. Have you ever sat down to a
stack of term papers or a mountain of examination papers?
Hours of reading are involved. If it weren't for a realization
that that is a necessary part of my responsibility, it could be
very monotonous. Knowing it is God's will delivers from
monotony.

Paul said the same thing: "Servants, obey in all things
your masters according to the flesh; not with eyeservice, as
menpleasers; but in singleness of heart, fearing God" (Col
3:22). *Fearing God.* The service that was rendered was to
be done as unto the Lord because it was God's will. Paul cou-
ples with this thought of obedience another parallel thought:
"Whatsoever ye do, do it heartily, as to the Lord, and not
unto men; knowing that of the Lord ye shall receive the
reward of the inheritance: for ye serve the Lord Christ"
(3:23-24). "Whatsoever ye do, do it heartily." We usually
think that this word *heartily* means to do something with all
your might. But Paul is also emphasizing that it should be
done with the heart. He's moving into the realm of the
affections, saying that what you do in serving your master,
you do because of your love for the Lord. Do it heartily, or
with your heart, as unto the Lord. He didn't say do it because you love your employer. Paul recognized that employers may be mean and cantankerous. Perhaps you find it hard

to love them, but you can love the Lord; so the heart must be involved in the matter of obedience. With the will you can obey the master; with the heart you can love the Lord. He said that whatsoever you do, do it as to the Lord, heartily, or from the heart, for you serve the Lord Christ.

Housewife, as you work in your home, do all that dusting and cooking because you are the Lord's servant, and this is the Lord's will. You serve the Lord Christ. If it's God will for you to be a housewife, then you are tested on how you perform a housewife's functions. If it's God's will for you to be a secretary, you are tested by what kind of a secretary you are. If in His will you are a student, you are tested by what God's will is for you today, what you do in school. If it is God's will for you to be in business, you are tested by what you do at the office. You are there as a servant of the Lord, no matter what He gives you to do; and your love for Him should transform that which is routine and burdensome and monotonous so that it becomes your joy. One of the secrets of dealing with monotony is to personalize that which you are doing. If you are doing it for an organization that's one thing. If you're doing it to please a person, that's something entirely different. I know that husbands couldn't employ somebody to do what housewives do from early morning to late at night—working around the house, in the kitchen, with the children, keeping the home going. Why do they do it? They are personalizing it. They are doing it for their husbands. They are doing it for their children. And what they couldn't be hired to do, they do out of love. Why did the apostle Paul endure all those beatings, stonings, imprisonments, shipwrecks, and the weariness of all his travels as outlined in 2 Corinthians 11? "The love of Christ constraineth us" (2 Co 5:14). He personalized all he did. Everything he did was to please a person. Why was Ezekiel lying bound 430 days? He was pleasing a person.

If you get this concept of pleasing a person into your daily routine, it will transform anything that you may called upon to go through. It matters not how often you have to go through it. You are doing it to please Him. And a person who is captivated by this thought of doing everything heartily as unto the Lord knows the joy of the Lord even in the most routine of circumstances. I find it quite impossible to put myself in the place of some people with their activities, and I'm quite sure that others find it impossible to put themselves in my place. But I do know this: when God calls a man, He enables that man. It is not God's purpose to make life drudgery. It isn't God who does that, we do that to ourselves. And when you serve God in the area to which He appoints you and serve heartily as unto the Lord to please Him, the same joy that Paul knew in his prison experiences, or that Daniel knew in the lion's den, or Ezekiel knew while tied up in the marketplace, will be your joy. If day by day and hour by hour you are in the place of obedience and are serving Him in that routine of life, the joy of the Lord, not monotony, will be your portion.

9

God's Answer to

THE PROBLEM OF RESENTMENT

EPHESIANS 4:17-32

You never saw a bitter resentful baby. A child or a young person cannot harbor a grudge for very long. But it is not uncommon to find an adult, especially an older adult, who has become embittered and resentful. There has been a deterioration within the person so that he who once was happy, gentle and forgiving has become set in a pattern of resentment and bitterness that refuses reconciliation. The Word of God speaks about this common problem of bitternes or resentment.

It seems that the tenor of our times is to pattern life after the cow, seeking to imitate the placidity of that beast. Thus only on the rarest occasions may one be stirred to any vehemence or anger. Many personality cults of our day have adopted that as the norm as though there is no place for anger in an individual's experience. But God has not made us like cows. Since He has endowed us with a capacity to love, of necessity there must be within that capacity the ability to manifest anger. If there were no possibility of showing anger there would be no possibility of manifesting love because anger is the response to wounded love. Anger is the rightful response to some wrong or injustice; and if there were no standards of right and of justice, there could be no anger. But because the Bible sets forth standards of

111

right and justice, there will be anger when one beholds violated rights or injustices.

Many people are surprised at reading the commandment in Ephesians 4:26: "Be ye angry." The first response to reading that is to look into the margin to see if there is an alternative reading or to see if a *not* has been omitted from the text, as though it were to read, "Do not be angry under any circumstance." But since anger is the response to an injured love or a violated right, the apostle Paul meant what he said and it was accurately translated, "Be ye angry." The person who is so insensitive to violated right or justice or wounded love that he cannot respond in anger, is less than a complete human being.

It has become a matter of grave concern to law-enforcement officers and to sociologists and psychologists that people can witness a crime being enacted on the street in a public place and lift no finger to help the assaulted one. Refusal to take part in any enforcement of law and the maintenance of order has led many to believe that the foundations of our society are crumbling, if they have not already fallen. The secular psychologist or sociologist recognizes that apathy in such a situation bespeaks a very low level of society. It is motivated by nothing more than self-preservation. The lack of the rightful response of anger that should move a person to do something evidences a deterioration within that person. A man who has any capacity to love, must be angry at times.

Though we are not dealing with the problem of anger, we are dealing with a problem that grows out of the ability to be angry: the problem of bitterness, resentment, and bearing a grudge. A grudge, or resentment, or bitterness is the unharvested fruit of anger. When the apostle said, "Be ye angry, and sin not," he was saying that one is to be angry since God has given him the capacity instinctively to react to that which is wrong or unlovely, but in his anger he is not to let it become a settled disposition so that his anger leads to sin. Be angry, but in manifesting your anger don't let it control, dominate, grip, and possess you, so that the anger with its resultant resentment, bitterness and grudges becomes the major factor of your disposition or personality. When anger becomes settled it moves into the realm of sin, and when anger is manifested because it is personalized it becomes sin. Thus, when an individual responds in a situation because of the way it affects him personally, his response has become sin; and when an individual gives way to this personalized resentment and bitterness he has gone beyond the command of Scripture, "Be ye angry" and has violated the second part of the commandment: "sin not" in his anger.

In dealing with the problems of bitterness, resentment, and harboring grudges—all of which are the results of prolonged anger—the first thing that the apostle suggests is: "Let not the sun go down upon your wrath" (v. 26). He set definite bounds as to how long you may be rightly angry or how long your rightful response to a situation may be maintained without moving into the area of sin. He said, "Do not [under any circumstances] let the sun go down upon your wrath." Anger, in the first place, must be of temporary duration. It must be short-lived. It must not be maintained past nightfall because when the sun sets and the person goes to bed with that anger, it settles and begins to gnaw and irritate and eat like a cancer with devastating effects upon the individual. The one who sleeps with his anger will wake with it in the morning and be a frustrated, bitter man. The individual is held responsible for his emotions, and Paul says that we are to guard this emotion and deal with and discharge it before we go to bed at night lest it become a settled disposition. The apostle recognizes that grudges must be nourished to be preserved or maintained. Unless that grudge is watered to keep it alive, it will dry up like grass under a midsummer sun. Paul says that any manifestation of anger is to be short-lived, it must not be kept alive nor prolonged because it is not the initial manifestation of anger that controls the disposition. It is the prolongation of that anger that alters the disposition, transforming the kindly, gentle, considerate individual into a mean, cantankerous man. Therefore, the apostle gives his first practical consideration: Stop nourishing your grudges, which is another way of saying, "let not the sun go down on your wrath." That principle is valid in a number of different areas of life. Keep the slate clean day by day.

Another principle is enunciated by the Lord in Matthew 5:23-24, where He is speaking concerning a devout, God-fearing individual who was on his way to the temple to offer the prescribed sacrifices of the law. The man recognized God's claim upon him and his obligation to God. This obligation was fulfilled in giving gifts and offering sacrifices to God. Then Christ said that if you bring your gift to the altar and, as you are approaching the altar, suddenly the Spirit of God brings to your remembrance that your brother has something against you because of what you did to him, "leave there thy gift before the altar, and go thy way." The one bringing a gift to the altar was bringing what God calls an unacceptable gift. The law provided for the offerings over above the tithes, gifts, and sacrifices as acts of worship, praise, thanksgiving, and even dedication. But God deemed this man's gift to be unacceptable because he had done something that had caused his brother to hold a grudge against him. Notice that it is not the offeree who is holding the grudge and is embittered. It is what this one has done to another that has caused the brother to be embittered.

Our Lord is very specific as to what this worshiper is to do: He is to leave his gifts and go his way. "First be reconciled to thy brother, and then come and offer thy gift." Notice that God did not express disinterest in the gift. He desired it, but He wanted it offered in the correct way with a heart that was right with God because there was no barrier between brother and brother. Perhaps we thought that Christ would say that if you have a grudge against somebody you ought to go to him. But He said that if you have done something that has caused a brother to hold a grudge against you, you have the responsibility to initiate action resulting in reconciliation. Until there is reconciliation between brothers, there can be no acceptable sacrifice offered to God. Reconciliation between God and the sinner, as it were, is broken because of the lack of reconciliation between brothers.

This gives another principle on how to deal with the problem of bitterness. Although you may not harbor bitterness against another, but it comes to your consciousness that you have offended another so that he is holding a grudge or harboring a bitter spirit toward you, your responsibility in the light of the teaching of God's Word is to initiate the reconciliatory act. You go to be reconciled to the brother because there is no service, no sacrifice, no gift that is acceptable to God as long as you have been responsible for this bitterness or grudge.

This supplements what Paul taught in Ephesians 4, for the brother holding the grudge obviously has let a number of suns set, and that has gone on and on. It takes two to effect a reconciliation. One can't do it. In order to experience forgiveness, there must be two: the one who forgives and the one who asks for forgiveness. If one brother has offended another and has generated bitterness, discord, or strife in his brother's heart, those feelings cannot be dissolved until the offender asks for forgiveness. Then forgiveness can be extended and the grudge relinquished. Though the apostle Paul tells the grieved individual, "Don't you let the sun

go down on your wrath," he says to the individual causing
grief, "You go to your brother and get it straightened out
with him, so that his grudge or bitterness will not continue
beyond nightfall."

A third principle affects the individual himself. The writer
of Hebrews says, "Follow peace with all men." The word
translated "follow" means to diligently pursue or to chase
after. "Follow peace with all men, and holiness, without
which no man shall see the Lord" (12:14). How do you
follow peace with all men? "Looking diligently lest any man
fail of the grace of God; lest any root of bitterness springing
up trouble you, and thereby many be defiled" (v. 15). The
apostle is reiterating what Paul said in Ephesians 4:3, that
we as believers have the responsibility of keeping the unity
of the Spirit in the bond of peace. What will disrupt the
unity of the body? Bitterness (v. 15). One brother has a
bitter attitude toward another brother. That bitterness will
affect not only the one holding the grudge and the one
against whom the grudge is held, but it will disrupt the whole
assembly and divide it by bitterness. Just as crab grass will
spread and take over a yard, one seed of bitterness that is
nourished, maintained, and kept alive will send out its shoots
or roots and defile many. The first one affected is the one in
whom the root of bitterness springs up. Then, after it has
troubled him, it will affect many.

A man can't hold a grudge and keep it to himself. It seems
utterly impossible. We've got to tell somebody else the wrong
done us. We explain why we're bitter; and we spread our
resentment in an ever widening circle. Then he gives an Old
Testament illustration: Esau, who despised his birthright.
All Esau had to inherit from his father was what God had
promised him. He didn't think God would be faithful to His
promise, and he counted God's word as being of no value.
When Jacob came to barter with him concerning his birth-

right, Esau's attitude was that the birthright had no value. But when he gave it to his brother, what happened? The root of bitterness began to grow in Esau, and he manifested animosity and hostility against Jacob until that household was divided. The father was on Esau's side, and the mother on Jacob's side. What was happening? Many were defiled. The root kept on growing when sometime later Jacob got his father's blessing in addition to the birthright. Then the root of bitterness that had been harbored over this extended period of time erupted. The next place Jacob was found was out by the brook, fleeing into the wilderness to put as much space as possible between Esau and himself. Esau was going to kill him, and he knew it; and the only thing he could do was flee. Those two brothers were brought to that position by a root of bitterness which sprang up, was nurtured, and finally erupted in dissension.

In 2 Samuel 15 is the record of Absalom's rebellion against his father. This striking young man led an open revolt against the honored King David, and almost all Israel went out after Absalom and forsook David. How could that have ever happened? In the preceding chapters Absalom had avenged the wrong done his sister and slew Amnon, David's son. David was angry with Absalom for taking the law into his hands and doing what the king should have done. His anger was justifiable; any other response would have denied any love that he had for Amnon. But Absalom fled and left the land. David's anger seethed and continued for days and months that stretched out to years, and finally Joash convinced David by subtle means that he was wrong in his unforgiving spirit and his failure to restore Absalom to the city. So David gave permission to bring Absalom back, and it seemed as though they were effecting a reconciliation. But then David hastened to add, "Let him turn to his own house, and let him not see my face" (2 Sa 14:24). The veiled threat was that if David saw him he would kill him. There was no forgiveness; the root of bitterness was growing and increasing. It was infesting not only David, but his household and whole kingdom.

And when the people saw his unforgiving spirit even after the passage of years, they did not want anything to do with the king who had become an embittered old man. They wanted Absalom. When Absalom presented himself as a judge, they were ready to make him king, because David's resentment and nurtured grudge had turned him from the sweet singer of Israel to a bitter man before whom they fled. David is an illustration of what the writer of the Hebrews says about a root of bitterness which may spring up and trouble you but won't stop there. Many shall be defiled. The honorable and esteemed and godly king David had to forsake the city of Jerusalem, his palace, his family, his throne, everything, to flee into the wilderness. Why? Because the root of bitterness had sprung up. That is why the apostle said in Hebrews 12:15 that the individual is to examine himself diligently to see if he is bitter, harboring a grudge, or has become resentful, and if that has become his settled disposition.

What does the writer mean when he says "lest any man fail of the grace of God . . ."? How does God's grace manifest itself? In forgiving sinners. When a man harbors a grudge against anyone, he is failing to extend to another the grace that God has already extended to him. So the apostle said that if you have received grace from God because God who was angry with sin has been satisfied and has extended the grace of forgiveness to you, you are to look diligently to manifest this same grace of forgiveness lest any root of bitterness springing up trouble you and "many thereby be defiled."

Paul commands in Ephesians 4:30, "Grieve not the holy Spirit of God." He is not saying, "grieve not the Holy Spirit," he is saying, "grieve not the holy spirit of God." "Holy" here is the characterization of the Spirit. He is the holy One. Then the apostle, speaking of that which grieves His holiness, speaks of some specific sins in that assembly that would grieve the Spirit who is the holy One. "Let all bitterness, and wrath, and anger, and clamour, and evil speaking, be put away from you, with all malice" (v. 31). How can verse 31 be reconciled with the "Be ye angry, and sin not" of verse 26? It is quite simple. Verse 26 is the rightful response to a manifest wrong, but verse 31 is the settled disposition of the one who had the right to be angry but did not follow the scriptural principles and terminate that anger before the sun went down, who refused to be reconciled with his brother, and who let that anger—rightful as it was—settle upon him so that in his speech he manifests bitterness and wrath and continuous outbursts of anger and loud talking against the one against whom he holds the grudge. Verse 31 describes a wicked, old man. That is what any child of God can become. If the root of bitterness is planted and nurtured, this is what you will become until the Spirit of God pulls up that root.

Resentment or bitterness expresses itself generally through the tongue. This is a matter of concern to the apostles writing in the New Testament. If we were to make up a catalog of sins today, these of Ephesians 4:31 would be put down at the bottom of the list as though they were inconsequential. But Paul emphasizes that to which we give so little attention. The greatest danger facing a church founded on the Word is not defection from doctrine, not disavowal of the authority of Scripture, nor a denial of the integrity of the Word of God. The greatest danger that faces that congregation is the misuse of the tongue. We let the sun go down on our wrath. It becomes a grudge. That grudge grows into resentment and that resentment becomes our settled disposition. That, more than anything else, could defile and destroy the unity of the

Spirit in the bond of peace. May the forgiveness that we have received from Christ, and the grace of God that was manifested to us, be manifested through us so that we will keep short accounts with God, not permit the sun to go down on our wrath, be reconciled with the brethren, and give diligent heed to ourselves, and so that our fellowship with one another and with the Father will not be destroyed.

10

God's Answer to

THE PROBLEM OF PRESSURE

MARK 6:30-44

Did you ever try to clean beef stew off the kitchen ceiling? During World War II a hardware dealer in our town whispered in my ear that he had unexpectedly received a pressure cooker and would let me buy it for my wife. In those days when we couldn't get such commodities, the man was doing me a favor in making it available to me. So I bought it and took it home. It was a great help. The cuts of beef we got then needed a pressure cooker to make them tender enough to eat. My wife was preparing a stew one day—and a bang and a call from the kitchen brought me running. The pressure cooker had blown up, and what was supposed to be in the cooker was on the ceiling. It had a safety valve that was supposed to let off the excess steam, but somehow that safety valve had become clogged, and the pressure built up until the little rubber plug that was the safety valve let go with a bang and that pot emptied itself through that quarter-inch hole.

Many of us have looked at the pressure cooker on the stove and have seen ourselves in that pot, for it seems sometimes as though the pressure builds up inside of us with an explosive force and that if something doesn't let go we will fly apart. Sometimes it seems all of our release valves have somehow malfunctioned so that we can't let off the steam, and we are looking for a safe place to blow apart in secret. The complexity of the life that we live certainly seals the safety valves for many people, and they are trying to devise something that will quiet the tensions and remove the pressures by embarking either on a course of exhausting relaxation or by submerging themselves in active work with disastrous results.

Does the Word of God have any suggestions to make concerning this twentieth-century problem? Is the Bible that up-to-date? Many are laboring under a misconception in regard to pressure for they refer to it as something from without which builds up the pressure within us. But pressure does not come from outside; it originates from inside the person. In other words, no person can put you under pressure. You are the only one who can do that to yourself. If there is pressure, it is generated from within. The pressures under which we labor are our responses to external circumstances, and the internal pressure comes from our response to that which of necessity is external. Thus, wives can stop blaming their husbands for the pressure that they are under; parents can stop blaming their children; employees can stop blaming the boss; citizens can stop blaming their country. The only one you can blame for the pressure under which you live is yourself. You've had such an easy out and have said, "If my circumstances were different, if my job were different, if my income were increased, etc., then these pressures would go." No, the pressure is your personal response to the exterior circumstance.

Note another fallacy. Pressure does not come because you have too much to do. Most of us instinctively respond to pressure by saying, "If I just didn't have so many demands made upon my time, or if I didn't have so much to do, I wouldn't be under pressure." Many people, when they refer to vacations, talk about how good it was to get away from the telephone. That is the one thing they constantly mention—getting away from the telephone. This reveals their concept that if I didn't have demands made on me then I could rest and relax and the pressure would be gone. But I do not believe that it can be supported that pressure comes from too much to do. Rather, it comes from a person's response to his obligations.

It's not what I have to do, but my attitude or my response to the things that are my obligation. In this connection we suffer from overload. Most pressure comes from overloading. Did you ever blow a fuse? New homes are wired with sufficient circuits so that we have almost forgotten what it is to have a blown fuse or a tripped circuit breaker. But in older homes with few circuits, fuses frequently blew. You could blame the wiring as much as you wanted to, but it wasn't the fault of the wiring. It was the fault of the individual who overloaded the wiring. Station wagons are wonderfully convenient, but if used as a truck they will break down. You can blame the station wagon, but it isn't its fault. It was designed to carry a certain load; and if you make it into a truck, you needn't be surprised if it breaks down. When there is a load limit and it is exceeded, you can expect a breakdown. I seem to be contradicting myself because I said a moment ago the pressure doesn't come from too much to do, and then I turn right around and talk about pressure coming from an overload. What I am trying to point out is this: an individual must know his capacity, his rate of load, and then adjust to that load. We put ourselves under pressure because we have not rightly related the load to the capacity or the work to what we are able to perform.

In the light of this, recall the familiar incident in our Lord's life referred to as the feeding of the 5,000. In the earlier part of Mark 6, Christ called twelve from the many disciples or learners who sat at His feet, and sent them out two by two.

He gave them power to perform miracles to confirm their message, and then they went out to minister throughout the land. There were innumerable opportunities for ministry, and countless needy individuals to whom they could minister. Their days and nights were consumed in their labors, for they were faithful and diligent to their responsibilities. At an appointed time, the twelve came back to meet with Christ. They were men under pressure—pressure of the ministry, pressures of responsibility, pressures placed upon them by the magnitude of human, physical, and spiritual need. "And the apostles gathered themselves together unto Jesus, and told him all things, both what they had done, and what they had taught" (v. 30). They told Him how busy they had been and how exhausted they were from the pressures.

Notice the Lord's first response: "He said unto them, Come ye yourselves apart into a desert place, and rest a while." One of the first solutions to the problem of pressure is to have a safety valve, and for these disciples the safety valve was to get away from the ministry, to get away from the multitude, to get away from the needs of suffering humanity and to be apart with Him. One quaintly put it this way: "If you don't come apart and rest, you will come apart." Christ was saying there was need for rest. Thus He took them out into the desert place even though needs were unmet, the multitudes were not healed, and the masses were still unconverted. He still said, "Come ye yourselves apart into a desert place, and rest a while." Rest was designed to be a safety valve, and He said in effect, "If you don't rest, then you'll have to be retired."

Taking them out into the desert represented a diversion. Can you think of anything more glorious than to be occupied in the ministry for the Lord, anything more thrilling than to announce throughout Israel that the Messiah had come? Anything more gratifying than to minister to the lame, and to the blind and the sick, and see immediate healing? And as gratifying and satisfying as that was, the Lord called them away from it and He said, "You need diversion." He recognized that they could not continue without interruption, in even that glorious ministry without coming apart, so He said, "Come apart before you come apart."

Frequently in the gospels when the Lord retreated from the multitudes to a secluded place, it was that He might give Himself to prayer. By so doing He was suggesting that not only physical rest from their labors and diversion from their ministry were necessary, but He was showing them that a personal intimate fellowship with the Lord was equally so. Prayer can have the greatest therapeutic value. On a great many occasions as I have engaged in a counseling ministry with people, I have found they will begin to pour out their problems in a volume of words; and all I can do is sit and nod to show them that I am listening and understanding. The tension has built up so that they have got to pour out their hearts. Often in telling me their problems, they begin to arrive at the solution to them. They have sought out one who would listen, and they are finding the therapeutic value in sharing their experience with an understanding listener. Now for an individual who is under pressure or in an inner turmoil, what better listener is there than God? What better listener than the High Priest who was touched with the feelings of our infirmities, who was tested in all points like as we are, yet without sin?

A professional counselor recently said that he had counseled a much smaller proportion of Roman Catholic than Protestants. He couldn't understand why (this man was evidently a stranger to all religions) until he had found the secret of the Catholic confessional. He said the individual who went to the confessional let off pressure to the priest's listening ear and was relieved of the burden, guilt, or pres-

sure of that which he had confessed and consequently didn't
need professional counseling. What the man did not see is
that there is no bona fide method of dealing with sin by telling it to the ear of an individual. You cannot be forgiven sin
by telling any man about it. But it was noteworthy that an
individual could be relieved from the pressures under which
he was operating by telling that which caused the pressure.

Our Lord was praying to set an example for these disciples
so they would turn over to the Father all that was a burden,
a care, or a concern to them; and, in telling an understanding
Father, they were relieving themselves of the built-up pressure. That simple act provides an important clue to God's
method of dealing with this problem of pressure. We must
have an open safety valve. There must be rest, there must
be diversion, and there must be communication with God.
One of our problems is that we allow this safety valve to
become clogged. We're willing to talk to somebody else
about our problems, but we do not talk to the source of all
strength, the one in whose arms there is rest and relief. And
because our communication with God is cut off, the pressures
mount. "Come ye yourselves apart . . . and rest a while."

When Christ took the disciples out into the desert, He did
not take them away from the problem. They boarded a ship
privately and thought they were leaving everything behind
as they made their way across the lake. But by the time they
had gotten the boat across, the whole multitude had gotten
around the lake and was waiting for them there. Thus, they
left the place of pressure but they didn't leave the cause of
it. It was still there. It is like the businessman who works
himself to exhaustion in the office from 8 to 5 and then takes
a briefcase home to work from 6 until midnight. He's out of
the office, but he isn't away from the pressures of work. If
you are trying to get away from pressure by changing your
geographical location, you will find the pressure is there, and

you'll face it there. It goes back to what we said previously. The pressure doesn't come from without. It comes from within, and the disciples faced the same multitudes with the same needs, and they had the same responsibilities that they had on the other side of the lake. There has to be some other answer.

The Lord commanded the disciples to make them "sit down by companies upon the green grass. And they sat down in ranks, by hundreds, and by fifties" (vv. 39-40). There was a job to be done, for Christ assumed the responsibility of feeding them. How did He go about it? He made the multitude number themselves off so that they were divided up into equal companies, which suggests that orderliness and discipline were involved in getting this job done. They had to plan. They had to organize, and then they had to carry out their work in an organized manner.

The principle that the Lord laid down here is that one of our great needs, if we are to keep from pressure, is to learn to arrange our work, plan our schedule, or budget our time so that we complete what has to be done in the allotted period of time. The difference between a man who can turn out a vast amount of work and the man who turns out only a little is not in the man's physical strength nor in his mental acumen, but in his ability to organize and discipline himself to get the job done. This is one area where we fail and put ourselves under such pressure. It is not the amount of work that we have to do, but the pressure that results from our attitude toward that work and which often is generated by our lack of planning to get the work done.

What are you going to do if there's just too much to do? Whose fault is it that you have so much to do? Probably one of the hardest words to learn to say is *no*, but this is imperative if we're to prevent an overload. Demands made on any individual will soon mount and far exceed what the individual can handle. It becomes necessary to decide whether we are compact station wagons or ten-ton trucks. If we decide that we are lightweight station wagons, then we'd better put a load limit; and if we would keep from pressure, we must refrain from assuming a responsibility that we cannot fill.

Often pressure results not because of the job that is to be done but because we feel inadequate for that job. If, during his presidency, former President Lyndon B. Johnson had stopped off in Dallas on one of his frequent trips to his Texas ranch and had told me, "I want you to come to Washington to become my administrative assistant," should I have accepted? I would have been under pressure because of my inadequacy. Not because he had asked me to work eighteen hours a day in Washington. The feeling of total inadequacy to meet that job would have put me under pressure, and my only sensible reply would have been to decline. Because I know that I am not suited for that job, I wouldn't last any time at all. A feeling of inadequacy, insecurity, or inferiority puts us under pressure, and yet pride insists that we say yes. We enjoy feeling flattered and honored when we're asked, even though we know all the time that we could not possibly do it.

There is a principle here for the child of God. God has given each of His children certain spiritual gifts; and if God has given us one gift and we try to exercise another gift, it is no wonder that we get under pressure because we are not equipped with the gifts to do that which we have assumed. God has given me some gifts. Other gifts God has given you. If you try to exercise my gift without possessing it, you would feel a pressure that I don't feel. Or if I conversely tried to do without your gifts what you are gifted to do, I would be under tremendous pressure. One has to evaluate his ministry, service, and work in the Lord's vineyard, not in the light of the invitations that come, but in the light of his gifts. And if he steps outside of the bounds within which God has given him gifts, he can expect pressure as the result. One practical way of handling this problem is to learn to say no. Christ said, "Sufficient unto the day is the evil thereof" (Mt 6:34). In more current terms: "Live one day at a time."

Most things that we worry about are not today's problems but tomorrow's. We delight to borrow from tomorrow. It is not today's problems that get us down; it is tomorrow's heaped upon us today. That is why the Lord said one day at a time—one hour at a time—one moment at a time. I would hate to start to walk from Dallas to New York City; I doubt if I could make it. But I can take one step at a time headed in that direction. That's all the Lord ever asks of us—one step at a time. And any person can take one step and then one more step.

When the disciples were given the commission, "Give ye them to eat" (Mk 6:37), they recognized their inadequacy and insufficiency. That recognition could have put them under unbearable pressure, but they weren't broken by the pressure of this responsibility. They waited until the Lord provided for them that with which they were to fulfill the obligations placed upon them. They put the five loaves and two fish in the Lord's hands, and He multiplied them in His own hands—not in the hands of the disciples, nor in the baskets that they carried. The multiplication was in the Lord's hands so that He was feeding the multitude. The disciples were only a channel for orderly distribution. This leads to a principle: when we are given a responsibility and work is pressed upon us, as God's children we can trust the Lord to enable us to do the work that He expects of us.

Pressure comes because we take the responsibility from His hands and stagger under its weight, bearing it ourselves instead of letting Him bear it. We take the load from the

Lord's shoulders and wonder that it staggers and crushes us. All that the disciples were asked to do was to take what they were able to bear from His hands and to distribute it to the needy. When we take the Lord's place and feel that the responsibility for the day's work is ours, we are subjecting ourselves to undue pressure because of our insufficiency. This applies to the man in the office or pulpit, or to the housewife or to the student in school. Whatever God has given us to do, it can put pressure on us in any area in which we move unless we are trusting His strength and faithfulness to perform that which He has given us to do. "As thy days, so shall thy strength be" (Deu 33:25). That is His principle. "They that wait upon the LORD shall renew their strength; they shall mount up with wings as eagles; they shall run, and not be weary; and they shall walk, and not faint" (Is 40:31). But who are the ones who can mount up and run and keep on walking? Those that wait upon the Lord! Had these disciples been out of contact with the Lord, had they assumed the responsibility of feeding this multitude, they would have succumbed to the pressure because of their woeful inadequacy. Imagine the frustration if they had tried to feed the multitude with five loaves and two fish! But when they turned it over to the Lord, He made it possible for them to do that which He had commanded. It was His power, provision, and grace that enabled them. The pressure was gone because the responsibility was the Lord's.

Stop trying to play God. Stop trying to take the place that He has reserved for Himself. Our Lord had to take these disciples apart and during their time with Him, show them that pressure was not relieved by getting out of work, but by learning that they could lean upon Him for strength for the work. Christ gathered that multitude together so that the disciples could have a visible demonstration of what the apostle Paul learned later, "My grace is sufficient for thee:

for my strength is made perfect in weakness" (2 Co 12:9). Rest, diversion and communion are all necessary. Remember that pressure is our response to external circumstance; and when we are rightly related to the Lord Jesus Christ and draw from His strength, plan with His wisdom, then operate by His power, strength will be given to discharge that which is His will.

11

God's Answer to

THE PROBLEM OF LONELINESS

2 TIMOTHY 4:6-18

Have you ever observed how many cartoons have their setting in some tiny, deserted island? Usually one or two castaways are shown under a palm tree. There seem to be almost endless variations as to the comments that can be made by the castaways in that situation. The psychologist would say that we see humor in such situations because at one time or another we all have felt as if we were cast away on a little island. We were in a sphere of loneliness where the world had passed us by; and we felt utterly forsaken, with no one to whom we could turn or upon whom we could depend. All of us are subject to loneliness, and God's Word gives some practical suggestions on God's answer to this problem.

Loneliness may arise from a number of different causes. It results when one is bereft of a loved one. It comes when one leaves familiar scenes and goes to strange places where he is unknown. Or loneliness may come because one has been forsaken by former companions because of his testimony for Christ. They have cut him off because he has turned to the Lord; and, in his desire to live for Christ, he is no longer acceptable in their society. But whatever the cause for the loneliness, we find that God has a care and a concern. Notice first that loneliness does not arise simply because of

132

the absence of people, because a crowd is often the loneliest of places. You who travel have experienced this. You are surrounded by people, and yet you feel the desolation of loneliness. For loneliness is not dependent upon the number of people with whom you may be in the same room or same place, but rather your relationship to those people. One can be utterly desolate and lonely in a crowd, or delivered completely from all loneliness with one person. One's relief does not depend upon the number of people, but rather, upon the relationship to a person.

In the Word of God are the stories of those who experienced times of loneliness and found solutions in their experiences. The prophet Elijah is a most interesting man to study because, as James says he "was a man subject to like passions as we are" (5:17). Jezebel had introduced a heathen god into Israel's religious life; and the nation, clamoring after some new thing, had been quick to espouse the queen's goddess. Ahab, in order to satisfy his new bride, installed her in a position of authority in religious affairs and, to please her, had erected a number of idols and temples to her god. He had declared the worship of Baal acceptable along with the worship of Jehovah. Then God had sent Elijah into the midst of that wicked and profligate court; and, with no equivocation, he had denounced their sin of turning from Jehovah. Elijah stood alone, surrounded by multitudes; he felt abandoned because none seemed to share his faith. When he was told that Jezebel was going to have his head as the price for his preaching, Elijah fled to the wilderness and hid. Coming to a cave, he lodged there. "Behold, the word of the LORD came to him, and he said unto him, What doest thou here, Elijah?" (1 Ki 19:9).

Elijah had been alone in the wilderness previously, but then he could at least anticipate the coming of a raven to feed him. He must have found some companionship even in

the raven, but there were no ravens here. Nothing but the
dark cave in which he was hiding. Feeling disconsolate and
defeated because he was standing so alone, his loneliness was
extremely real. As God began dealing with Elijah's problem
of loneliness, first of all He revealed Himself to the prophet.
Elijah had to learn the lesson that a man who knows the
Lord is never alone because God has promised that He will
be a very present help in time of trouble. This was the beginning of the solution of Elijah's problem. He had to learn
to "practice the presence" of Jehovah. And in the darkness
and the loneliness of that cave was God. He had been there
all the time. Elijah had not withdrawn from God; he had
withdrawn unto God, although he didn't realize it. He was
not finding God. God was revealing Himself to the prophet
in his loneliness. Elijah was so disconsolate that he didn't
seem to have the capacity to pray to find God or to get out
the scrolls and search them to find God. His loneliness and
despair had robbed him of all spiritual initiative, and God
came to him then to reveal His presence to him.

God revealed Himself in spectacular ways. He said, "What
are you doing here, Elijah?" The prophet said he had been
very jealous for the Lord God of hosts and for the people to
whom he had been sent to minister, but that his message had
been rejected and he had been rejected and now they were
seeking his life. There he was—abandoned and rejected by
men, a lonely individual. To be wrapped in his loneliness
was not the end for the prophet, so God took him out of that
cave and put him upon a mount. Then God began to deal
with him. "The Lord passed by, and a great and strong
wind rent the mountains, and brake in pieces the rocks before
the Lord" (v. 11). This was a manifestation of God's power,
but it was not a manifestation of His personal presence.
Elijah could have no sense of fellowship with a God whose
might was likened to an earth-splitting tornado or hurricane.

If God had been that, the prophet would have wanted to run and hide in the cave to get away from Him, for he could feel no sense of personal fellowship with a God of such irresistible might.

After the wind there was an earthquake, and the finger of God split the mount on which the prophet was standing. But once again Elijah's heart would not respond to a manifestation of God's power because power is an impersonal thing and a person was not made to fellowship with the impersonal. He was made to fellowship with and respond to a person. So after God revealed His power, which was to show the prophet that God was able to take care of Jezebel and all the messengers that she sent, God revealed His presence. The verse has become so familiar: "after the fire a still small voice." There God revealed His personal presence, and the prophet was able to enter into fellowship with a God who was personally present. So he wrapped his face in his mantle as a sign of humiliation and of worship because he was unworthy to stand in the presence of a holy and a righteous God. Then God communed with him again and said, "What doest thou here, Elijah?" This sense of the personal presence of Jehovah, the mighty God, was the initial step in dispelling his loneliness. Elijah could no longer say, "I am alone," because when he had a revelation of God's personal presence with him, he could say, "God and I are together here." The fact that he was personally and intimately in fellowship with God would dispel the loneliness because it did not require a thousand people and Elijah, but only God and Elijah to dispel the loneliness.

This principle is illustrated on a number of occasions. In Deuteronomy 31:6-8 is a brief portion of Moses' charge to Joshua. Moses was about to be received into glory, and Joshua was to assume command over Israel. Moses said, "Be strong and of a good courage, fear not, nor be afraid of them: for the LORD thy God, he it is that doth go with thee; he will not fail thee, nor forsake thee. And the LORD, he it is that doth go before thee; he will be with thee, he will not fail thee, neither forsake thee: fear not, neither be dismayed" (vv. 6, 8). Notice that twice it is promised that God will not forsake Joshua. Moses had told Joshua that he was departing; and a sense of loneliness must have swept over Joshua because he had been depending on the strength, counsel, wisdom, and guidance of Moses. Now the one on whom he had leaned was about to be taken away, and Joshua probably said, "I'll be alone. I'll have no one to guide me, no one to lean on, no one to direct me. And the mantle of Moses, that giant of Israel, is about to be placed on my shoulders." No doubt that mantle brought a deep sense of loneliness to Joshua. But Moses said to Joshua, "The Lord will not forsake thee; he will not fail thee, neither will he leave thee." Joshua's sense of loneliness was to be dispelled by the promise that God would not leave him alone. God and Joshua could lead the people into the promised land.

The prophet Isaiah was sent to the nation Israel to give them comfort in a desolate hour because God was about to send the people into captivity, and they would suffer under Gentile bondage. Isaiah had ministered in the courts and given counsel to King Hezekiah. But he could not change the message that there would be judgment from God, and Hezekiah's heart was gripped with loneliness because he felt that God in judging them would abandon them. Hezekiah was a lonely man, but Isaiah came to give this word: "Fear thou not; for I am with thee: be not dismayed; for I am thy God: I will strengthen thee; yea, I will help thee; yea, I will uphold thee with the right hand of my righteousness" (Is 41:10). And again he said, "Fear not: for I am with thee" (Is 43:5). Notice in both these passages that Isaiah is promising that God's personal presence will be with those who trust in Him; and when God is personally present, a man who senses and appropriates that presence has a power in his experience and need not be swept away in loneliness.

If there were a man who had a right to be lonely, it was David. In 2 Samuel he had been set apart by God to be king of Israel; but he was despised and hated and rejected by Saul, and Saul had sought again and again to put him to death. So it was necessary for David to leave his friend Jonathan and to flee out into the wilderness and live alone. But this is what David testifies: "I have been young, and now am old; yet have I not seen the righteous forsaken, nor his seed begging bread. For the LORD loveth judgment, and forsaketh not his saints" (Ps 37:25, 28). David could look back even to his lonely experience in the wilderness and testify that God was with him and that God had provided his physical food and had preserved him. As he looked back over the days of his life, he could say, "The LORD . . . forsaketh not his saints."

Christ's disciples considered themselves orphans when the one on whom they had leaned for help was going away from them. For more than three years the Lord had nurtured, supplied, guided, and taught them. He was as a father to them, and they had had no care or concern for any physical or spiritual need because He had faithfully provided. And when He told them that He was leaving, loneliness gripped them. But our Lord said, "I will not leave you as orphans" (Jn 14:18, NASB). He called them orphans because of the loneliness that they felt. At that time there were eleven of them. Eleven men ought to be able to band together and dispel loneliness. But our Lord said, "I know the loneliness that grips your heart." He promised them: "Let not your heart be troubled; ye believe in God, believe also in me. In my Father's house are many mansions: if it were not so, I would have told you. I go to prepare a place for you. And if I go and prepare a place for you, I will come again, and receive you unto myself" (Jn 14:1-3). He promised, "My Father will come and dwell with you, and I will come and dwell with you." The solution to their problem of loneliness was God's personal presence with them. The gospel of Matthew closes with "Lo, I am with you alway, even unto the end of the earth." Where can you go and get away from His presence? Elijah tried it in a cave and found Him there. David tried it in the wilderness and found Him there. The disciples thought they had lost Him in the crowds of Jerusalem, but He was there. "Lo, I am with you alway, even unto the end of the world."

How does this compare with Elijah's experience? Notice that God's provision for these lonely men was the same as that which He provided for Elijah: the revelation of His personal presence with them. We recognize that Jesus Christ is the infinite, eternal Son of God. We acknowledge that at the time of His ascension He was received up into glory, and was seated at the right hand of the Father. But almost every time we begin to pray to the Father or to the Son, we try to think our way across an infinite expanse of space to come into the presence of God the Father or God the Son. The trouble is, we have missed the blessed truth that God the Father, God the Son, and God the Holy Spirit have taken up residence in the body of the person who has accepted Jesus Christ as his personal Saviour. The Father, Son, and Holy Spirit are dwelling in God's temple. They are as near to you as you are to yourself; yet, we have never learned to live with this vital, living presence of the triune God within. Christ said in the upper-room discourse in John 14, and He repeated it again and again, that "we will come and make our abode with you. We will dwell with you." Thus we can never be alone. And if we can never be alone, the only reason we experience loneliness is that we have not practiced the presence of the Lord; and God's first solution to Elijah's problem was to reveal His presence to Him.

Notice a second thing in 1 Kings 19:15:

> And the LORD said unto him, Go, return on thy way to the wilderness of Damascus: and when thou comest, anoint Hazael to be king over Syria.

The prophet was told in verses 16-18 that there was a ministry for him to perform and that he shouldn't be hiding in a cave. He was to be busy doing that which was God's will for him. This brings it down to a very practical level: when one is occupied with doing God's will, he can sense God's presence and approval within. Activity in discharging God's will is one of the best antidotes to loneliness. It seems as though in the "good ol' days" when "man had to work from sun to sun and woman's work was never done," there simply was no time to nurse loneliness, as we have time to do today. One of our problems is how to deal with time; and when we permit ourselves to be engrossed with ourselves instead of being occupied with the will of God, then we are subject to this temptation of loneliness. Idleness is not God's will for a person. Granted, sometimes God lays a man aside and puts him to bed and he can't do anything but stay there; and obviously that is in His will. But idleness is not a part of God's will because there are always those who can be told of His love and grace. There is always that which can be done as a discharge of the spiritual gift that God has given us. When one is occupied with the will of God as Elijah was told to be, he will be delivered from the loneliness that grips him.

There is a third suggestion in verse 18: "Yet I have left me seven thousand in Israel, all the knees which have not bowed unto Baal, and every mouth which hath not kissed him." Elijah was lonely because he thought he was the only one

who loved God. But God told him in a most practical way
to go out and find some others who loved the Lord, the same
Lord he loved. In finding those with a similar faith and a
similar love for the Lord, there would be fellowship and companionship that would keep him from the loneliness he was
experiencing alone in the cave. This is so elementary that it
scarcely seems necessary to mention it, but many give way
to loneliness simply because they do not take the time nor
the opportunity to cultivate those of like precious faith in
order that they might be delivered from this feeling which
could defeat them. God's personal presence was to be the
foundation. Built on that was to be Elijah's activity in the
discharge of God's will. Then would come his companionship with those who loved God. These are God's practical
solutions in 1 Kings 19 to this common problem of loneliness.

A good deal that is written in a popular vein about loneliness begins by telling a lonely one to get busy: Do something, occupy yourselves, keep your hands busy. But that
is starting on entirely the wrong basis. Notice that God
didn't first tell the prophet to get busy and find some friends,
and he would get over his loneliness. God began with the
revelation of His personal presence. All the busyness and
all the friendships that you can establish apart from Christ's
personal presence will never satisfy this need.

Paul's experience recorded in 2 Timothy 4 paralleled that
of Elijah, and the same principles were involved. Paul had
been shut up in the Roman prison, which probably was the
second time he had been imprisoned in Rome. In writing to
the Philippians after his first imprisonment he was certain
that he would be released from jail; but in this second imprisonment there was no expectation of relief—he was anticipating an early death. Paul was surrounded by the Roman
military legion, by the guards that held him; and yet Paul in
that prison was a lonely man. This is obvious when he sug-

gests to Timothy, "Do thy diligence to come shortly unto me" (v. 9). Timothy was a beloved son in the faith, and Paul wanted Timothy to be with him because of the loneliness of his heart; so he asked Timothy to come as quickly as possible. He wanted Timothy because he had been forsaken by those who once were with him and he refers in verse 10 to the fact that Demas had forsaken him and had gone to Thessalonica, and Crescens had gone to Galatia, Titus and other companions to Dalmatia, and Luke his physician was the only one who was with him (vv. 10-11). He also wanted him to bring Mark along because he could find companionship with him. He refers to the fact that in his defense of the faith he had to stand absolutely alone. We see his loneliness in verse 16; and here a note of pathos creeps into Paul's letter: "At my first answer no man stood with me."

This reference to his "first answer" probably refers to the procedure at a Roman trial. There had to be an indictment before he could have been brought to the actual trial, and Paul had already had this preliminary examination by Roman officials, and that was his first answer before a Roman court. The next step would be the actual trial itself, and Paul was actually saying, "I was brought in to answer the indictment brought against me, and I looked for someone to stand there with me to identify himself with me so I wouldn't be absolutely alone," but he says, "no man stood with me, but all men forsook me." This seems to include all the men mentioned in verses 10 and 11 that had previously been Paul's traveling companions. When it came time to appear in the Roman court, it seems to suggest, they were afraid, and abandoned Paul. But Paul was strengthened in that loneliness: "The Lord stood with me, and strengthened me" (v. 17). Paul's help, as well as the solution to his problem of loneliness, was the personal presence of the Lord. When Paul looked over that crowded courtroom and didn't see a familiar face, he knew that the Lord was right there with him, and he was strengthened in his loneliness by the Lord's personal presence.

Paul also requested companionship. There were still those who had not bowed the knee, so he asked Timothy to come and to bring Mark. And Paul was looking for these human companions. But meanwhile there was work for him to do. What could he possibly do in prison? A suggestion is in verse 13: "The cloak that I left at Troas with Carpus, when thou comest, bring with thee, and the books, but especially the parchments." Students who have just completed a semester's study will not find this particularly attractive, but Paul wanted to study. For him study was a discharge of God's will. He couldn't be out evangelizing, but he could be studying. Only books that were most precious were written on parchment because of the expense, and the parchments to which he referred may very well have been the Old Testament scriptures. Paul could not preach, but he could give himself to God's Word. And in thus giving himself, he was sustained. The Lord's personal presence, the presence of companions, and his study in the Scriptures sustained him.

Perhaps one person is the loneliest figure in all the Word of God. Under the olive trees on the slopes of Gethsemane He cried out, "Not my will, but thine be done." And on Calvary where He was left alone, He cried, "My God, my God, why hast thou forsaken me?" That which was in the mind and heart of our Lord is described in Psalm 22. In His loneliness, Christ cast Himself upon God: "I was cast upon thee from the womb: thou art my God from my mother's belly. Be not far from me; for trouble is near; for there is none to help" (Ps 22:10-11). What was He claiming in His loneliness? The Father's presence. Even though God had forsaken Him because He was made sin for us, yet it was the presence of the Father that would sustain Him. "Be not far from me . . . for there is none to help." Then along with His plea for God's presence, there was praise for the victory that He anticipated from God: "I will declare thy name unto my brethren: in the midst of the congregation will I praise thee. For he hath not despised nor abhorred the affliction of the afflicted; neither hath he hid his face from him; but when he cried unto him, he heard. My praise shall be of thee in the great congregation: I will pay my vows before them that fear him" (vv. 22, 24-25). In His loneliness there was trust and praise: trust in a God who could not fail, and praise that God would bring Him out of that dark hour into the light of His face.

God's answer to the problem of loneliness is to realize and appropriate the blessed truth that God the Father, God the Son, and God the Holy Spirit have taken up residence in God's child, and thus God is personally present; and where God dwells there need be no loneliness. God has a will. We may be occupied in that will; and in doing that will, there is relief from loneliness. Through fellowship with those of like love and like faith, there is deliverance from loneliness. When one is occupied with God and the Scriptures, then indeed God will deliver from loneliness. May we experience His personal presence so that we shall be delivered when we are tempted to wrap the mantle of loneliness about us and hide away like Elijah in our caves.

12

God's Answer to

THE PROBLEM OF INFERIORITY

JEREMIAH 1:1-10

Among the problems we face in day-to-day living, few are any more distressing or defeating than the problem of inferiority—or what is called today an inferiority complex. That this is a prevalent problem is evident by the mass of literature being published in book form and periodicals. Popular treatments in the realm of psychology deal with it continually. Many books that try to tell us how to win friends and influence people are merely explaining how to overcome feelings of insecurity, a sense of inadequacy, a fear of failure, a sense of embarrassment at meeting strangers, the self-consciousness that grips us when we have to stand in front of others and speak. These feelings plague men in the business world, who often fight these problems as they try to get ahead in business. We fight these problems in our Christian testimony and witness, for we feel under compulsion to tell others of Christ, but we fear people and we fear failure and we feel our own inadequacy and insufficiency, so we keep our mouths shut.

The Word of God has some suggestions about this very problem. Normally we don't want to admit that we feel inferior because we like to give the impression of being secure and of feeling adequate for any situation. Yet, if we were honest, most of us would have to say that we face that

144

problem. Have you ever been called upon to speak before
people and you felt nervous and jittery and fidgety when you
thought about getting up? That is a sign of inferiority. When
you got ready to speak and found that your hands were
dripping wet, that nervousness was a sign of inferiority. You
were very careful about the clothes that you put on because
you wanted to make just the right impression upon people.
That very care may arise from a desire to impress people
because you feel inadequate for the occasion.

A member of my congregation, upon learning that I would
discuss the problem of inferiority, said, "I didn't know any-
body had that anymore." Sometimes we feel that we need
to emphasize Romans 12:3, "Let no man think of himself
more highly than he ought to think" for there is danger in
pride, but for this study we say, "Let no man think *less* of
himself than he ought to think." One is just as much a problem as the other. It is just as wrong for a man to think less
of himself than he ought to think as it is to think more highly
of himself than he ought to think. Either will destroy his
effectiveness as a Christian witness or as a servant of Jesus
Christ, and both are prevalent problems.

Many of God's choicest servants at one time or another
seemed to be plagued with this problem and had to overcome
it before they could become effective in the ministry to which
they were called. Several illustrations in God's Word point
out this problem. Jeremiah is a good starting place because
in his discourse with God he goes to the root of this problem
of inferiority. It arises from a fear of people. That was the
first basic underlying cause of Jeremiah's inferiority. God
said to him, "Be not afraid of their faces" (1:8). Jeremiah
felt so inadequate, so insufficient and so self-conscious when
God set him apart to this ministry as His prophet that he
immediately took cognizance of the people to whom he
would minister, and he regarded their superior position. Con-

sidering who they were and what they were, he was gripped by a fear of them. But God put His finger on the root of the problem and told Jeremiah he was succumbing to these feelings of inferiority and inadequacy because he was afraid of their faces.

At that time Israel was in a period of apostasy and declension. Judgment had been pronounced upon the nation, and Jeremiah was being sent in order to announce the judgment and to warn the people of the impending doom: "Then the word of the LORD came unto me, saying, Before I formed thee in the belly I knew thee; and before thou camest forth out of the womb I sanctified thee, and I ordained thee a prophet unto the nations" (1:4-5). Jeremiah did not aspire to this ministry nor prepare himself for it; he was appointed by God. Nothing in Jeremiah caused God to select him, for he was appointed to this ministry before he was born.

But this was Jeremiah's reply: "Ah, Lord GOD! Behold, I cannot speak: for I am a child" (v. 6). He felt inadequate because of his youth and because of his immaturity in the things of this life and the affairs of this world. Without doubt, those to whom he would go would be the elders in Israel. Elders were those who had been put in positions of directing and administering the national affairs. They were responsible people, and their responsibility had not come without the passing of years; so not only were they responsible men, but they were mature in years. Jeremiah was a young man, probably in his late teens or early twenties, although his age is not given. This was a tremendous responsibility to be placed upon such a young man, and yet God did the appointing. But young Jeremiah didn't look at the One who commissioned. He didn't consider the word of the One who sent him. Instead he looked upon those elders to whom he must go and, anticipating their words of ridicule and reproach, he told God, "I can't go. I'm inferior. I'm inadequate because of my youth." Obviously he lacked maturity in years. Part of wisdom is for a young person to recognize and admit his inadequacy and immaturity because this is difficult for young people to do. But Jeremiah was not revealing his wisdom. He was totally gripped by fear and by feelings of inadequacy and insufficiency. He was afraid of their faces and, discounting the God who sent him and being occupied only with those to whom he was to minister, he said, "I cannot speak: for I am a child."

In order to deal with Jeremiah's fear of people because of his youth, God gave him a promise: "I am with thee to deliver thee" (v. 8). To deliver him from what? Why, the elders—those to whom he would go and minister. God said that he didn't have to be afraid of them because He would deliver him, for "I have put my words in thy mouth" (v. 9). God would protect him from their mouths, and He would put something in his mouth that would shut their mouths. Clearly, Jeremiah wasn't afraid of what those elders would do; he was afraid of what they would say. Nothing stifles Christian witnessing as much as the fear of what "they will say." These words "they will say" have probably defeated more Christians than any others. Why are we so concerned about what they will say? It is because we are so concerned about our reputation. We want to build ourselves up in their eyes. Our fear is because of our feelings of inferiority. We draw back from doing anything that would give them cause to belittle us. Thus inferiority came to Jeremiah because of fear of people and because of his youth, and God's answer was to promise him deliverance and protection, and to give him His own word to speak.

Another prophet, Amos, was not brought up in a court. He did not have the advantages of a fine education as, for instance, Ezekiel or Daniel had. Nor did he have the privileges of wealth. Amos was called to be a prophet when he was a sheepherder, and a gatherer of sycamore fruit. The sycamore fruit is very much like a fig and is hard and inedible unless when it is ripening somebody squeezes it to make it edible. And so, the gatherer of the sycamore fruit spent his time out among the trees squeezing fruit. He combined two jobs. He could look out for the sheep while he was squeezing fruit. This is a very unlikely background from which to call a prophet. But God called Amos and sent him from Judea, where he had been ministering, up to the northern kingdom. He was a southerner going north, and he wasn't very welcome. Those in Israel listened to Amos condemn them for their sin, and they said, "We don't like what you say. If you want to prophesy, why don't you go back home and preach there? There is sin there." Amaziah told him, "O thou seer, go, flee thee away into the land of Judah, and there eat bread, and prophesy there: but prophesy not again, any more at Beth-el: for it is the king's chapel, and it is the king's court" (Amos 7:12).

Amos preached a message where it could count most—in the king's hearing. He proclaimed his message in Bethel, the capital of the northern kingdom, and in the king's palace. The king and his court rejected the message, which would be enough to give any man an inferiority complex. Amos recognized that he did not have the training to be a prophet. Samuel, called by God to be a minister to Israel, had established a school of the prophets where he and his successors trained young men. These students were called the "sons of the prophets," and they were being prepared by the man of God for a ministry in the truth of God. Because he had not attended that school of the prophets, Amos sensed that he did not have the necessary educational background that would equip him to be a prophet. And when Amaziah said to Amos, "If you want to preach, go down to Judah where you came from," Amos' reply was, "I was no prophet, neither was I a prophet's son; but I was an herdman, and a gatherer of sycomore fruit: And the LORD took me as I followed the flock, and the LORD said unto me, Go, prophesy unto my people Israel. Now therefore hear thou the word of the LORD" (7:14-16).

Amos might have pleaded lack of preparation, lack of formal training in the things of God and have been silent because of this lack of preparation. He had this basis for his inferiority. But a degree from a school is no prerequisite to effectiveness as a witness for Jesus Christ. No school can give a man spiritual gifts. It may equip a man to use the gifts that God has given him, but any individual who is sensitive to the Spirit of God and who is diligent and faithful in his own study in God's Word can be effective as a witness for Christ. Some of the most effective witnesses and personal workers have never set foot on a campus for formal training for the ministry. And yet, many of us give way to an inferiority complex and refuse to be a witness for Christ, pleading what Amos might have pleaded: "I was no prophet. Neither was I a prophet's son. I had no formal training, no formal schooling. Please excuse me from discharging that which the apostle Paul placed upon all believers—to be ambassadors for Jesus Christ." Whereas Jeremiah's fear of people arose out of a feeling of his immaturity, Amos' arose out of a feeling of inadequacy in preparation.

But God said to him, "Go, prophesy unto my people Israel." Amos didn't go because he felt prepared. He didn't feel prepared and he wasn't prepared. But Amos went because God told him to go. If a child of God considers only his own formal schooling in the things of the Scripture, he will succumb to this feeling of insecurity and inadequacy; and he will say that his lack of schooling exempts him from fulfilling the Great Commission, "Go ye into all the world, and preach the gospel to every creature" (Mk 16:15).

Moses had the finest educational background that the world could afford in his day. All of the treasures of Egypt were at his disposal. Material wealth was his. Brought up as the son of pharaoh's daughter, he had all that the Egyptian court could possibly confer upon him. If there ever was a person who had no excuse for an inferiority complex it was Moses, but he had one. His inferiority arose out of feeling of a lack of personal qualifications for the work being entrusted to him. Moses didn't have the same problem as Jeremiah because he was at least forty years of age when God called him. Nor was his problem the same as that of Amos: no preparation, because he had had all the schooling that they could give in Egypt. But he had the problem of feeling he lacked personal qualifications. God said to Moses, "Come now therefore, and I will send thee unto Pharaoh, that thou mayest bring forth my people the children of Israel out of Egypt" (Ex 3:10). What a responsibility was being placed by God upon this man! "And Moses said unto God, Who am I, that I should go unto Pharaoh, and that I should bring forth the children of Israel out of Egypt?" (v. 11). Moses felt he lacked personal qualifications because he missed a vital point. He was only the human instrument through which God would do the delivering; he was not the deliverer. God was the deliverer, but Moses felt personally inadequate because he assumed a responsibility God had not given him. Instead of recognizing himself only as the instrument, he thought that he would have to be the deliverer. This explains his reply to God: "Who am I?" It was true that he could not deliver, but God gave him the solution to his problem: "And he said, Certainly I will be with thee; and this shall be a token unto thee, that I have sent thee: When thou hast brought forth the people out of Egypt, ye shall serve God upon this mountain" (v. 12). God told Moses that He would do the delivering and that Moses was the instrument He would use. Further, God promised Moses His presence, and the solution to Moses' inferiority was found in the personal presence of God. God said, "I will be with thee." God's solution to Jeremiah's feeling of inferiority was a divine call. To Amos' feeling because of a lack of preparation, God gave a divine message. And with Moses and his feeling of a lack of personal qualification, it was a divine presence that was to deliver fear of people.

There was a second basis for a feeling of inferiority in Moses. He said to God, "Behold, they will not believe me, nor hearken unto my voice: for they will say, The LORD hath not appeared unto thee" (4:1). In the first place, Moses, like Amos and Jeremiah, felt inferior because of a fear of people; but second, he felt inferior because of a fear of failure. And that is a second major contributing factor to an inferiority complex. We don't want to try anything or venture anything for God because of a fear of failure. He was afraid of ridicule. He was afraid they would not hearken nor believe him. He was afraid of rejection. He was afraid they would not hearken unto his voice. His fear of ridicule and fear of rejection spelled out only one thing: failure. He felt it was better not to try anything than to try something and fail in it. Today we put a great store upon success, and a man is judged by his successes. Many men have no successes because a fear of failure has always prevented them from trying anything. Behind nearly every success is a multitude of failures which the person experienced before achieving success. This fear of failure keeps men from venturing anything. If God had not intervened in Moses' experience, Moses would have said, "I'll not venture anything for God because I'm afraid I might fail. Therefore, I'll do nothing."

The cult of success today has elevated success all out of proportion; as God's representatives we need to recognize this fact. God has never promised us success in the Word of God. In fact, He's warned us repeatedly that we face failure. Christ told the disciples as He was getting ready to thrust them out into the ministry, "Don't expect success because the world is going to hate you, persecute you and reject you and reject your word." What would happen if a commencement speaker stood up today and told the graduates, "Every last one of you is doomed to failure!" What a commencement address that would be. At least it would be remembered. That was Christ's commencement address because He told His disciples they would be failures in the eyes of the world. God views things in quite a different way than the world. We think that when we give a word for Jesus Christ or bear testimony for Him, that if the person doesn't receive Christ the first time we speak to him, we're a failure. So we say, "I'll just keep my mouth shut rather than fail again." But God hasn't told us to speak the word with a view of being a success or having the message received. He tells us to speak the word so that He might be glorified through the word that is spoken, whether it is received or not. That fear of failure turns us into spiritual cowards, causing us to suffer the same feeling of inferiority that dissuaded Moses from the path of obedience. God had to turn the rod in Moses' hand into a serpent and restore it to a rod, He had to cause Moses to put his hand into his cloak and bring it out leprous, and He had to promise him that He could turn the water into blood before Moses would trust Him. The answer to Moses' problem of fear of failure was to trust God to accomplish His own purpose through him.

How can we handle this problem of inferiority when we recognize its presence in us? Each illustration cited has this in common: each person suffered from the feeling of inferiority because he was occupied with himself. And if we are to overcome inferiority, we must stop being occupied with and concerned about ourselves, making ourselves the center of

attention. Do you ever have a problem remembering names
when you are introduced to people? Do you know why?
You probably were thinking so much about what kind of an
impression you were making on them, you didn't even hear
their name. What are we saying? Simply that the root of
the problem of inferiority is the problem of self. We're concerned with self; our whole life revolves around self. We
always want to present ourselves in the very best light. So
we think, If I do this what will they think? If I say this,
what will they say? If I do this, what will the response be?
We are thinking in terms of ourselves all the time. This is
where the flesh has to be reckoned to be dead to Christ because it is the dominating force within us that produces this
feeling of inferiority.

Another practical thing is not only do we have to stop being occupied with ourselves, but we must stop hiding behind
our fear and our excuses and trust God for the victories that
He has promised. Jeremiah was hiding behind an excuse:
I'm too young. Amos could hide behind an excuse: I haven't
had the education. Moses could hide behind an excuse:
After all, I was brought up in a court, and I've lost all contact with these people, and I'm personally inadequate. They
all had excuses, but those excuses produced an inferiority
complex in these men. If we are to conquer this problem,
we must stop hiding behind our fears and excuses, and start
trusting God to do that which He said He would do when
He called us for a specific task. Many people know that the
gospel is the truth that Christ died for our sins according to
the Scriptures, and that He was buried, and that He rose
again the third day according to the Scriptures. Since you
know the gospel, how many people have you ever told the
gospel? Why haven't you? Perhaps you're using Jeremiah's
excuse and claiming to be too young. But bearing witness
to the truth is not a matter of age; it's a matter of obedience

to God's command to share that which we know. Many of us have said that if we had more education we would be a good witness for Christ. But we are hiding behind Amos' excuse because men need to know just one thing: that they are sinners and that Christ died for sinners. We know that, and we're withholding the truth from them. The flesh has control and has reduced us to this inferior position and has sealed our lips. We must quit hiding behind these fears and excuses and start trusting God for the victory.

Another truth is to be noted. The apostle Paul says that a man ought "not to think of himself more highly than he ought to think" (Ro 12:3). The reason he gives for why we should not have an inflated view of ourselves is the same reason we should not have deflated views of ourselves, for Paul goes on to deal with spiritual gifts (vv. 4-8). This is a very vital truth in the whole problem of inferiority. God the Holy Spirit at the time a person is saved gives a person some spiritual gift. This gift is that which may be exercised by the child of God for the good of the whole body of believers. Some gifts seem outstanding and others of less significance. There are gifts for the edifying of the body, the church, such as apostles, prophets, evangelists, pastors and teachers. Other gifts might be deemed lesser gifts: the gift of helps, the gift of government, the gift of hospitality, the gift of giving. But every assembly of believers needs all these gifts, and every believer has some gift to use for building up the body and for equipping the saints. No man receives a gift by coveting it, praying for it, or training for it. The gift is given by God.

Every gift is essential and necessary. One has no basis for feeling superior to another who has some other gift; nor do you have the right to feel inferior to others because you seem to have a lesser gift. Therefore, if you do not have a gift that puts you in the public light, this does not mean that you are inferior in the body of Christ, or that your gift is unnecessary or that you are inferior. There is no such thing as an insignificant gift. Paul reminds us that as in this human body we have many members and all members have not the same office, so we being many are one body in Christ (Ro 12:4-5). All believers are one body, and we have gifts that differ. No person should feel insignificant or inferior because God has given him a gift that is to be exercised quietly. My responsibility before the Lord is to exercise the gift that God has given me by the Spirit's power and to His glory, and the responsibility God has placed upon you is to exercise the gift God has given you. When one recognizes that his gift is from God and that God expects him to use that gift, he is delivered from this feeling of personal inferiority.

God has made us His sons. You may not have been born into a family of high social position. You may not have been born into a family that can give you a great material inheritance. You may not find employment that will give you great monetary reward. You may not have graduated from a prestigious school. But you are a child of God, and what could be higher? But you belittle the name of Jesus Christ when you as God's son belittle yourself before men out of fear of a person or fear of failure. As a minister of the gospel of Jesus Christ, I feel I can hold my head higher than any king or president who walks this earth. I am an ambassador of Jesus Christ. Why should I fear men? And you are Christ's ambassador. You are His personal representative. Why let fear of men or fear of failure cause you to drag the name of Christ down to the level of your inferiority? As the song writer put it,

> I'm a child of the King, a child of the King:
> With Jesus my Savior, I'm a child of the King.

This is not intended to produce pride. But there is a difference between pride and a recognition of what a person is in

Jesus Christ. We are not asking you to become proud, but to recognize your position as a child of the King and to find deliverance from inferiority because of what you are in Jesus Christ.

13

God's Answer to

THE PROBLEM OF KNOWING
THE WILL OF GOD

JUDGES 6:33-40

We are living in a day of synthetics. Natural products seem to be unavailable. We walk in shoes made out of synthetics on carpets that are made out of synthetics. We wear clothing made out of synthetics. In this day of synthetics, Gideon's fleece seems a very scarce commodity.

Many of God's children are in constant perplexity; they are concerned about doing the will of God, but they're ignorant as to how to determine His will in their daily experience. This is a very important problem for we recognize that unless we are rightly related to the will of God, we can know nothing of His joy, peace, and victory. It would be so simple if we could put out a fleece at eventide, go to sleep, and wake up in the morning and have an unquestioned answer to the revelation of the will of God as Gideon did. In the morning when Gideon woke up he had the answer—incontrovertible, incontestable, certain. Many of us in our insecurity cry out today, "If only God were dealing with us the same way He dealt in Gideon's day so we could determine His will."

A great deal has been written on knowing God's will, and the abundance of literature proves the interest of God's people in this subject. But, even after reading much of the

157

literature on this subject, we come away still asking the question, "How can I know the will of God?" Often the steps given are so intricate and detailed that we feel we can't follow them. Thus we cannot find God's will for ourselves. That leads many to trust someone else for guidance, so they come to the pastor or some trusted friend and ask him to find God's will for them. His guidance may be wrong because God does not reveal to one individual His will for another. The apostle Peter inquired what the Lord's will was for John. The Lord said, to put it bluntly, "It's none of your business, because that's a personal and individual matter between us. You be interested in God's will for you and forget about God's will for somebody else." This is one of the most personal and intimate relationships which the child of God can sustain to his Lord, and if we have not learned some of the biblical principles for determining God's will, we certainly will be adrift on a sea without charts, compass, or star to guide.

Before a person can understand God's will for him, he must have a right attitude toward God's will while he is seeking it. For unless he has the right attitude toward God's will, he will never discover it. Christ stated a principle that applies here. He had been teaching the nation, declaring the truths of God's Word with clarity, power, and certainty. He had authenticated the truth that He presented by the miracles that He performed. But the Jews to whom He ministered couldn't understand the truths that He taught.

And the Jews marvelled, saying, How knoweth this man letters, having never learned? Jesus answered them, and said, My doctrine [my teaching] is not mine, but his that sent me. [That is, I didn't originate the truths that I am teaching, but they are His that sent me. Now notice this principle:] If any man will do his will [or, to adopt the marginal reading which is preferable, "If any man willeth

to do his will" or, if a man is first willing to do His will],
he shall know of the doctrine [teaching], whether it be of
God, or whether I speak of myself (Jn 7:15-17).

Christ is speaking primarily concerning the truth that He
sought to impart, and He said that an unwillingness to
receive the truth precludes a man from understanding the
truth being taught. A man whose mind is closed to the truth
that is presented will never benefit, no matter how positively
or straightforwardly or logically the truth is presented. An
individual must be willing to be taught before he can learn
anything.

Discovering the Lord's will is determined by the same principle. If any man is willing to do God's will, then he shall
know it. An individual who says to God, "I'm not certain
whether I'll do Your will when I know what it is, but You
reveal Your will to me and let me decide what I'm going to
do about it," is never going to know God's will. God does
not reveal His will to His child so that he can debate about
it and decide what he is going to do with it. God's will is not
revealed to be debated, but to be obeyed. Christ is giving a
very vital principle: until the child of God settles in his own
mind that he is committed to doing God's will—no matter
what it may be—God will not reveal His will to him in any
detail at all. There may be generalities, but there will never
be specifics. Thus this is the primary prerequisite to knowing
God's will: unreserved committal to God's will, no matter
what it is, before we can expect a revelation of that will.

One of the most important passages in the New Testament
is Romans 12:1, "I beseech you therefore, brethren, by the
mercies of God, that ye present your bodies a living sacrifice."
The presentation of oneself to Christ as a living sacrifice is
the surrender of one's individual will to a new Master. Christ
looked at those who addressed Him as Lord when He walked
among men, and He said, "Why call ye me Lord, Lord, and

do not that which I say?" (Lk 6:46). The apostle Paul is emphasizing the fact that God requires His child to present himself to God without restriction and without reservation, and only after that commitment is made to Christ does God tell His child what He wants him to do. There is a difference between recognizing Christ as Saviour and submitting to Him as Lord or Master. When one comes to Christ as Saviour, he comes to deal with the sin question. When he submits himself unreservedly to Christ as Master, he is dealing with the question of an obstinate, stubborn will, and he is submitting himself to God's will. Many who have accepted Christ as Saviour have never recognized the concomitant obligation to surrender the control of their lives to Him. We like to feel that in certain areas we are sovereign, and we say, "I am willing to do this and this, but I am not willing to do that and that." Many who go into the Lord's work say, "Lord, I am perfectly willing to be a pastor or a teacher, but don't ever ask me to go to the mission field." They are telling God what they will and won't do. Don't expect God to tell you what He wants you to do when you hold out those reservations. Until you are willing to say to Him, "I will do what You want me to do," He will not reveal His will to you. There must be an unreserved commitment to His will before we can expect any details of that will.

At this point Christians run into the greatest problem. Failure in this area produces the greatest unrest in the Christian life, because every day believers arise and debate again God's will for them. They go through agony and turmoil every day trying to decide what they are going to do. They suffer constant agitation, defeat, and frustration because this one cardinal issue has never been settled. How much different it is to commit oneself once and for all to the will of God—whatever it may be—and then get up in the morning without facing a debate about doing His will because yesterday that issue was settled. When you settle that question, you'll get up in the morning with the attitude, "I am going to do God's will whatever it is today." The debate has already been settled. That once-and-for-all committal of the will to God has removed the necessity of this incessant debate. That is why the apostle exhorted the believers to present themselves once and for all to the Lord Jesus Christ. There must be a scriptural attitude toward God's will before we can expect a revelation of it. But when one submits himself to the Lord to do His will, God begins to unfold step by step that which is His will for His child. Get this cardinal fact in mind: God can speak loud enough to make a willing soul hear, but God cannot speak loud enough to reveal His will to an unwilling soul. Willingness to do God's will is a prerequisite to knowing that will.

The second thing to be emphasized is the relationship of the Word of God to His will. The psalmist says, "Thy word is a lamp unto my feet, and a light unto my path" (119:105). The lamp and the light are the revelation of God's will for the individual. The psalmist is saying that the Word is the revelation of God's will. Gideon needed a fleece because so very little of the Word of God had been written, and without the Word he could not determine God's will. We don't need a fleece today because we have the Bible. God accommodated Himself to the paucity of revelation in Gideon's case; but, with the completion of revelation, Gideon's fleece is no longer necessary because the Word of God is for you what the fleece was for Gideon. God's will is revealed in His Word. God's will is God's Word, and God's Word is God's will.

The vast majority of our problems for which we seek God's will are already settled for us in the Word. We often view His will as though it were hidden and veiled, but most of which we seek to know is already revealed in the Word. This means that we must know the Word of God before we can determine His will. If God has already revealed His will in this book, why would He give a special revelation concerning His will? He won't do that because He has already settled that issue.

Recently I talked to a young man who was convinced that he knew God's will concerning the girl he was to marry. He professed to be a believer in Jesus Christ, and the girl to whom he had become engaged happened to be an unbeliever, so much so that she had told him that church would have no place in their marriage. The young man came to me to discuss his forthcoming marriage. He was convinced it was God's will for him to marry this girl. But how could it be God's will when the Word of God specifically declares that it is contrary to His will for a believer to marry an unbeliever? That issue is settled; the Word is unequivocal on that. Why did he come to me to try to find out God's will in the matter when the Word settled it?

Answers to many of our problems are in the Word. Associations in the business world are covered in the Word. Social relationships are covered in the Word. Our practices and pleasures are settled in the Word. Why ask if it is all right to do this or that when the Word of God settles it? Don't raise that as a question as though it weren't revealed. It's already settled. Therefore, one must study the Word in order to know God's will because His will for an individual will never be contrary to the Word. The will of God is the Word of God, and the Word of God is the will of God. So, there must not only be the right attitude toward the complete will of God, unquestioned committal to His will, whatever it may be—but there must be the right relationship to the Word.

Coupled with the Word of God there will be the testimony of the Holy Spirit to guide into God's will. This might be called an inner conviction. There is a certitude within us, in which we feel convinced that such and such is God's will for us as individuals. I can remember the night when I was only nine or ten when God the Holy Spirit spoke to me and called me into the ministry. If someone had asked me to explain it, I couldn't have done it. I know I didn't hear a voice, but God spoke to me. There was an inner conviction. From that time on, I knew that there was no other course that I could follow. There was certainty in it. The Spirit Himself, who bears witness with our spirit that we are the sons of God, will also bear witness with our spirit confirming what the Word says concerning God's will for us. So the child of God who would know God's will must be rightly related to the Holy Spirit. One who is insensitive to the Spirit's prompting and convicting will never understand nor know God's will. Nor will the one living with a grieved Spirit, nor the one who has quenched or stifled the Spirit, nor the one who denies the Spirit's right to lead him regarding God's will. Thus, there must not only be the right relationship to God's will and Word, but there must be the right relationship to God's Spirit.

When God's Word and Spirit agree on any course of action, we can be certain that it is God's will, and the product of conformity to His Word and Spirit will be the peace of God. This is what Paul mentions in writing about understanding the will of God: "Let the peace of God rule in your hearts, to the which also ye are called in one body; and be ye thankful" (Col 3:15). The word translated "rule" is a Greek word that means to be a referee or umpire. Let the peace of God umpire or do the deciding in your heart. This is what the apostle is teaching. Suppose you read God's Word and feel prompted by His Spirit to do a certain thing, but when you begin to execute that which you felt the Word and the Spirit directed you to do, you have a restlessness of heart. Then you had better be very careful because the Spirit may be convicting you that somewhere, somehow, you have misread or misinterpreted the Word.

The Holy Spirit is not the author of confusion; He is not the author of restlessness. He is the author of peace; and one who is in the will of God and is doing the will of God, will have the peace of God as his settled portion. We have to be very careful at this point to determine the origin of the restlessness. As the will of God is revealed in the Word and by the Spirit, my old nature may rebel against doing it and may produce restlessness. We must determine the source of the restlessness. Is it the old nature rebelling against God's will or is God the Holy Spirit taking away peace?

Then, conversely, we must be careful if we have peace in doing a certain thing because that peace may not be coming from the Spirit of God. The peace may come from the old nature that wanted to do that thing, and we've convinced ourselves it's the right thing to do and it makes us happy to do it because it pleases us. We mistake the complacency of the flesh for the peace of God. Therefore, we must be very careful about making this rule of peace the only determinative factor because the flesh can give peace, or doing something that pleases us can give us a false or pseudo peace. We've got to be very careful that it is the Spirit of God who gives the peace, and not the flesh. Convincing themselves that what they want to do is right, many people say they have the peace of God. But don't ever feel that the peace that you have in doing something is God's peace if that action is contrary to the Word. His blessing and direction will be upon that which is His will.

Yet another factor must be emphasized in this matter of knowing God's will; it is the truth that it is God's responsibility to reveal His will to His child. Much is said about *seeking* God's will, but God's will is not so much something to be sought as it is something to be received. If it is my responsibility to seek God's will, then that suggests that His will is hidden and veiled, and only by diligent search can I ever find it. How different that is from waiting for God to reveal His will to His child, which is His responsibility. Then it is the child's responsibility to obey what is revealed. Coupled with this fact is the great need for patience. We ask God to reveal His will to us, but we get no lightning flashes out of the blue, no thunderbolts, nor an earthquake. Then we conclude that God has not revealed His will to us. But how could God more clearly reveal to you to keep right on doing what you are doing? God's will does not necessarily mean change, but you're suggesting that God's will always means a change of direction. Obviously you cannot conceive that God will set you on a path and keep you on it. And when you seek His will or when you are waiting for Him to reveal His will, the proper attitude would be for you to keep on with what you are doing until God changes the course of direction. Only when He makes that change is a change indicated. God's will is not necessarily concerned only with changes. If you have received God's will and He has set you in the course of that will, then God is interested in your continuation in that same path, not a change of direction. But many of God's children are burdened by this misconception that God's will means a change, and if they've been going in the same direction for more than a week, they think they are out of His will.

There is need for a settled conviction that one is in God's will. Then there must be patient endurance and a continuation in that will. We should not constantly be asking for a change of direction, but should constantly and patiently continue in doing that which God has revealed. Many of God's children lack patience. They may feel that some change of direction is indicated. They feel that God is obligated to reveal a new direction immediately. If God doesn't, they panic and jump. If you are going to jump, you had better be very sure that the parachute harness is fastened securely! Many of God's children leap into the dark and end up in utter confusion. They have missed the point that it is God's responsibility to reveal His will and that it is dangerous to move until God indicates the time and direction.

Finding God's will is not some complicated process. It is not something so involved that only a spiritual giant could ever determine His will. God asks of His child a once-and-for-all commitment of his life to His will, whatever may be. When he makes that decision objectively, committing himself to do God's will, no matter what it may be, he settles the issue of his relationship to God's will and opens himself to the revelation of that will. He searches the Word to find the will. He walks step by step in faith and in constant dependence upon the Holy Spirit, trusting Him to guide and direct him into God's will. He has turned his anxiety about finding the will of God over to the one who is responsible to guide. When God sets him in motion and then seems to be silent, he keeps right on in that same straight course until God changes his direction because he is committed to doing God's will.

Child of God, give up this frustrating search for God's will and commit yourself to the one who's responsibility it is to reveal His will. Saturate yourself with His Word, and walk patiently in the path He directs. Gideon was a man who was afraid of taking one step outside the will of God. He asked God to guide him, and when God made His will certain to Gideon, the debate was over. Gideon took up his sword and his battle horn and obeyed. This was complete, unreserved commitment to God's revealed will. May this be your experience.

14

God's Answer to

THE PROBLEM OF LIVING FOR CHRIST IN THE BUSINESS WORLD

LUKE 16:1-13

The world watched as two American astronauts made their way from the earth into outer space, landed on the moon, and then returned safely back again. Although we talk about these men having been in outer space, if we stop and think for a few minutes, we realize that they were not really in outer space at all. A great deal of the investment of time and material was spent in keeping them in the atmosphere to which they were accustomed. For if they had actually gotten out of this earth's atmosphere for even a moment, they would have been dead. Much effort was put forth to keep the cabin atmosphere in which these men rode just the same as here on earth. When the hatch was opened and the man stepped out of the capsule into space, his body was not really in space. Thousands of dollars had been spent on a suit to keep him in the atmosphere to which he was accustomed, and inside of that suit there was an identical atmosphere to that here on the earth. He was surrounded by a hostile environment, but all care had been taken to maintain him in that environment in the atmosphere in which he had been born and which was necessary to support life.

When a child of God steps out into the business world, he is stepping from the atmosphere which he has been brought by the new birth into a completely foreign and destructive atmosphere. And unless he is insulated against that atmosphere, there will be a catastrophe. The problem that the believer has when he steps out into the business world is the problem of living the life of Christ in a hostile environment. He needs the same care to maintain spiritual life in that hostile atmosphere that the astronaut needed to step out of the capsule into the vacuum of outer space.

In dealing with this problem, Christ did not mince any words. He gave this categorical statement: "No servant can serve two masters: for either he will hate the one, and love the other; or else he will hold to the one, and despise the other. Ye cannot serve God and mammon" (Lk 16:13). The word "mammon" means this life with all that it holds, offers and contains. The word "mammon" means far more than just money. It includes all that this world has to offer. Christ said, "Ye cannot serve God and the business world at the same time." The background of our Lord's teaching is indeed significant. He spent much of His time in conflict with the religious leaders of His day, and Israel's religious life was dominated largely by the Pharisees, the official interpreters of the law. They were the traditionalists who reverenced the law of Moses and showed their reverence for that law by accumulating all the traditions of men and all the teaching of past rabbis as to what the law meant. And one of their basic concepts was that God put a great deal of store on material things and rewarded good men by making them rich. The Pharisaic attitude toward money was summarized by the simple statement: "Whom the Lord loveth, He maketh rich." That showed their whole attitude toward material things. Coveting God's approval, they coveted money as an outward sign of His approval, and they were ostentatious in their display of their material wealth. They gave themselves over completely to seek material things, to impress people with their goodness and godliness by showing how rich they were. Yet the Pharisees set aside the requirements of the law, the demands of righteousness. They rejected the concept of approach to God through sacrifice and invented a new approach through the outward observances of Jewish tradition. Our Lord constantly emphasized money in His teaching, trying to show them its true value and men's relationship to it. The Pharisees had had a stewardship because they were leaders. When God makes a man a leader he is responsible to God for that trust, for that stewardship entrusted to him.

The Pharisees had been unfaithful to their trust, and Christ told a parable in order to show the proper use of influence, of material substance, and of privileges and responsibility. He told the story of a steward—a man entrusted with the oversight of all the resources of a wealthy man—who was faithless in his stewardship and was about to be discharged from his office. His future prospects were grim. Obviously no other man would trust him with his material wealth, so he couldn't get another job as an estate administrator. The alternative was to turn to manual labor, but his only callouses were on the tips of his fingers from counting money and that hardly qualified him to take up a pick or shovel to go to work. The other alternative was to don the rags of a beggar and sit along the roadside and beg for alms, but he could not conceive of himself in such a position. He was too soft to work and too proud to beg. But he did have a short period left as the administrator of this wealthy man's estate, so he decided to use his position to prepare a place for him when he was discharged. He called together all his employer's debtors and he said to one, "How much do you owe my master?" And the man said, "A hundred measures of oil." He said,

"Sit down quickly and cut your bill in half. Make a new bill and write it for fifty." I don't know why he said, "Sit down quickly and write," because any man who was told to cut his bill in half would do it immediately without being told! And he called the next one in and asked, "How much do you owe?" He said, "A hundred measures of wheat." The steward said, "I'll give you a 20 percent reduction. Take off 20 percent; you only owe 80 percent." As each debtor came before this administrator and had his bill reduced, he became a new friend who would be glad to accept this man into his home when he lost his job.

The Lord was not condoning the underhandedness and deceitfulness of this administrator. What He was showing was that this man used his position of trust and responsibility to prepare for the days ahead. He then made it very clear as He explained that the children of this world are sometimes wiser than the children of light because the worldling knows that he has to prepare for the future and the children of light are often lackadaisical in business affairs and do not use their privileges and responsibilities with a view to God's approval. Christ taught that they were to be faithful in the trust given them so that when they stood before God to be judged for the stewardship, they would be received into glory and have a reward for their faithfulness. He was showing the proper use of material things, influence, power, and position.

Christ concluded His teaching by showing that there are two spheres which are mutually exclusive. "No servant can serve two masters: for either he will hate the one, and love the other; or else he will hold to the one, and despise the other. Ye cannot served God and mammon." Notice that Christ is categorical, saying there is a line of cleavage drawn between the things of God and the things of mammon, between the things of God and the business world, and that you cannot serve both at the same time. When Christ used the word "serve," He did not say a believer could not be employed. That was far from His thought. God gave work to man as a blessing. It was instituted in the garden of Eden. Even before the fall, Adam had work to do, and work was one of God's beneficial provisions for man. His work was made arduous after the fall in that he had to work by the sweat of his brow, but it was still God's gracious provision for man. God kept men busy with work that they might be kept from sin. Our Lord is saying here, "You cannot give yourself completely to God as a master and at the same time give yourself completely to business as a master." And when He used the word "serve" He was using it in the sense of that which is a controlling, dominating factor in a man's life. God and business cannot be preeminent at the same time. It is impossible to have two preeminent things because the word "preeminent" means "the highest." You can't have two highests. One or the other has to be in a place of preeminence. You cannot give yourselves completely to God and at the same time make your business the dominating factor in your life because you will either hate the one and love the other or else you will hold to one and despise the other. Therefore, you cannot serve God and man.

Like many of our Lord's statements, this is a hard saying. We would like to narrow it down to where we could be good men in the business world and good men in the church at the same time, making them compatible and serving God on Sunday and serving business the other five days of the week, and having Saturdays for ourselves or for our wives. But He says that is impossible. You cannot make the business world, or God, or even your wife, preeminent all at the same time. We are forced to a choice. The goals that God has for His child are summarized in Romans 8:29, "to be conformed to the image of his Son." God's purpose or goal for His child is to reproduce Himself in His child; and all that God does in the life of His child He does to reproduce His Son in that child.

Did you ever hear of such a goal in the business world? How different are its goals. Business operates for the products that can be produced and for the profits from those products. It operates with a view to expansion. The goal of business is success, and each business has its own measurement of success. We are not antibusiness. We are not preaching Communist propaganda, nor against capitalism. We can't operate the Lord's business except from profits. But the goals that the business world sets for itself are in contradistinction to the goals that God sets for His child; and if one is faithful to the pursuits of the business world, he cannot be faithful to the goal that God has set for His child.

There is a contrast between God and mammon in the methods by which the goals are produced, because God's method is to reproduce His Son by the power of the Holy Spirit. "It is God which worketh in you both to will and to do of his good pleasure" (Phil 2:13). Those who mingle in the business world know that, for the average business, anything goes that produces success; and because the methods of the Spirit are in contradistinction to the methods employed by the business world today, it is impossible to serve God and mammon.

These two spheres are mutually exclusive because God has His standards and ethics, and the business world has its own. The standard that God sets for His child is the righteousness of Christ, and the Scripture classifies as sin anything that is unbecoming to God's holiness. In the business world, whatever promotes success becomes legitimate and is accepted as ethical because the end is considered to justify the means. Scandal after scandal has been seen in high places because the business or the political world accepted the expediency that anything that promoted or produced the desired goals or success was acceptable and legitimate. And when Christ said, "Ye cannot serve God and mammon," He recognized that as far as the goals, methods, standards or ethics are concerned, God and mammon operate in two different spheres.

Another thing which needs emphasizing in this connection is in Christ's word in John 15. The world hates the believer, and it is a fact that the business world hates the child of God. Christ prepared the believers for that as He said, "If the world hate you [and it will], ye know that it hated me before it hated you" (v. 18). He was stressing that the world's hatred for the believer is only a continuation of its hatred of Christ. He gave at least three reasons why the world would hate the believers. First, "If ye were of the world, the world would love his own" (v. 19a). If you had your origin in the world, the world would love you because you have a common origin. "But because ye are not of the world, but I have chosen you out of the world, therefore the world hateth you" (v. 19b). In any organization a man may be accepted and may enjoy companionship with the other members of that organization until for some reason he decides to forsake it. Then all fellowship is immediately broken, and bitterness, rancor, and hatred are directed against the one who voluntarily left. As long as a man is in the world and operating according to its goals, methods and standards, that man is acceptable to the world; but just as soon as he comes to know Christ as his Saviour and is saved out of any relationship to the world and has adopted a new set of goals, standards and methods by which he conducts his life, the world can no longer tolerate him in their midst. The world will hate him because he is no longer a part of them. He has been chosen out and therefore hated.

Christ's second reason why the world would hate the believer is: "But all these things will they do unto you for my name's sake" (v. 21). If the world could vent its hatred against Christ personally, they would do so; but you are more accessible than Christ, therefore, you become a good substitute, and the world demonstrates its hatred of Christ by venting that hatred against you.

Christ gives a third reason why the world would hate the believer: "If I had not come and spoken unto them, they had not had sin: but now they have no cloke [covering or pretext] for their sin" (v. 22). Because the believer operates by a new standard, with new methods and for a new purpose, he convicts the unbeliever with whom he associates day by day. That unbeliever recognizes that he is not acceptable to God. He knows the believer has something he lacks, and he is miserable because the believer has it and he doesn't. He is reproached because he sees lived before his eyes a new kind of life according to new standards, and something within him bears witness of the fact that it is an acceptable standard to God. He cannot measure up to it or attain it, and therefore, being convicted by the believer in his midst, he turns against that believer in hatred. That is the only emotional response open to the unbeliever convicted by the believer.

God sent the prophet Isaiah with a message, "Comfort ye, comfort ye my people." Somehow we've been led to believe that we believers have been sent into the world to make the world comfortable. That is a lie of the devil. We have been sent into the world to make it miserable by living according to a different standard and rule, and following a different practice for different goals. The world is convicted and made miserable by the believer who conforms to the righteousness of Christ in his daily conduct. Salt in a wound hurts. They don't want to feel miserable; therefore, they hate you for making them miserable in their sins. These are the facts we face. When a man steps out into the business world, he is going into a hostile atmosphere. It is the sphere in which he once lived, but he has been redeemed from it by the blood

of Christ. He's going into a world characterized by hatred of
Christ and of those who trust in Christ.

How can the Christian man or woman who has to mingle
in this atmosphere exist? Every man has to make a choice
(see Lk 16:13). This is paramount. Students are looking
ahead to the days when they will be getting established in
some business, and those who are already in the business
world must make a choice. It is a choice of masters. It is a
choice as to whether you are going to serve God or to serve
business, the business world, and the material things which
that world has to offer. If it were possible for you to serve
both, it would be of little consequence that you heed. But
because the Word of God says they are mutually exclusive,
you are faced with a choice as to whether God is going to
rule and dominate your life or whether business is going to
be the preeminent thing. Before you make a snap decision,
remember that a choice to serve God, to make Him preeminent, involves tremendous costs. Many of God's children
fail here, for they say, "It costs too much, and I'm not willing
to pay it." So often we think like natural men, above everything else we want to be successful in life. And we measure
success as the world does in terms of our income, the house
we live in, the clothes we wear, the school which our children
attend, and our responsibilities in the business world. These
become the marks of successful man. And since we are determined to be successful, we will pay any price to attain that
goal. Few put God first and make Him preeminent in life,
letting Him work out His will in them; few define success in
life as God does rather than as the world defines it. And the
businessman who moves out into the business world, to conform to God's goals and methods and standards at whatever
the cost and to make God preeminent in his life must be prepared to suffer for Christ's sake.

Suffering for Christ's sake is the norm; it's not the exception. Most of us would say that suffering for Christ's sake today in Christian America is the abnormal thing, not the normal thing. It has become abnormal because our lives as Christians are abnormal. If we were living the normal Christian life before men that God expected us to live so that every day our lives reproached unbelievers, we would have the response that Christ predicted in Luke 16. The man determined to make Christ preeminent in the business world must be prepared to pay the price or to suffer for Christ's sake. He will be hated; his faith will be ridiculed. His scrupulous observance of God's standards and his refusal to tamper or to play around with things that are unethical or immoral in the light of God's Word will never be accepted in the business world. One price that the businessman who is determined to be pleasing to Christ will almost inevitably have to pay is that when promotion time comes, someone else will be tapped for that promotion, not the man who has been out and out for Christ. There may be exceptions; you may be employed in a Christian organization. But that is the exception and not the rule. I have talked recently to several men who because of their diligence in maintaining a Christian testimony have been bypassed in promotions, and they all were told that the only reason was because they did not fit the organization. That is a price that a man must be prepared to pay if he is going to maintain a Christian testimony in the business world.

A man is in this business world out of necessity. He has the responsibility of providing for a wife and a family. In it he has a responsibility to God. Peter says, "Having your conversation [or manner of life] honest among the Gentiles: that, whereas they speak against you as evildoers, they may by your good works, which they shall behold, glorify God in the day of visitation" (1 Pe 2:12). The first responsibility that God places upon the man who lives in this hostile world is for him to maintain such honesty and integrity of character before his unsaved business associates that they may be directed toward God by that manner of life. That is what Peter means when he says "they may by your good works, which they shall behold, glorify God in the day of visitation." If the businessman goes from church on Sunday into the office on Monday and, because the boss tells him to, follows the ungodly boss' ethics and standards and practices, he will lose every possible vestige of testimony because he will have compromised his position before God. Peter says, "You be so honest in your manner of life that this man will be convicted and convinced and will find Christ as the Saviour, and in the day of judgment will glorify God for your life in his midst." Then he adds something else: "Servants, be subject to your masters with all fear" (v. 18). Or put it this way: "Employees, be in submission to your employers with all fear, not only to the good in general, but also to the froward [or the mean]. For this is thankworthy, if a man for conscience toward God endure grief, suffering wrongfully. For what glory is it, if, when ye be buffeted for your faults, ye shall take it patiently?" (2:18-20). If you make a mistake and your boss bawls you out, that is what you should expect, for it was your mistake. But if the boss blows his stack because of your godliness, and you accept that patiently, this is acceptable with God. This faithfulness in the responsibility placed upon us will itself be a testimony to the godless man with whom we have to rub shoulders in the business world.

Years ago when I was a seminary student and seeking employment, I went to a business firm and was given a job. I was told to report for work at a certain office, and there one of the owners had me sit down across the desk from him and he told me two things. First he said, "I'm putting you out on the rod-making machine because the man that will work next to you is unsaved, and I hope that you may have an opportunity to speak to him about Christ and give him a testimony." Then he looked at me and said, "You are a Christian, and we expect more of Christians around here than of non-Christians." I never forgot that, and I think he was right. Having a testimony to maintain will produce a faithfulness that will render a man unreproachable with those with whom he has to work day by day.

Another thing which must be considered arises out of Christ's teaching in a parable in Luke 16. Whatever we have to do in our business contacts and relationships, we are to do it as unto the Lord. The job may seem menial, but if it is God's will for you, it is to be done as unto the Lord, just as much as you would expect your pastor to do his job faithfully as unto the Lord. Because it is God's will for you to be in business does not mean that God has a different standard of faithfulness for you than He has for one who handles the Word of God from day to day and week to week. The same standard of faithfulness applies, and "whatsover thy hand findeth to do, do it with all thy might [diligence]" (Ec 9:10). What God expects of a man who is engaged day after day in the business world is, first of all, faithfulness to his employment and to his employer, that he might be irreproachable before that unsaved employer. God expects a man to maintain such a careful testimony that his employer will be brought face to face with his own relationship to Jesus Christ by the conduct. He doesn't necessarily say a word, but by his conduct he confronts his employer with Christ.

God expects us to face the decision as to who will be lord or master in life. For young people, this may mean a decision before you start out, and what a blessed thing it would be if at this point in your life you could determine that you would serve the Lord faithfully and that you would do His will faithfully and that you would faithfully conform to His goals, methods and practices so that your whole life will be directed toward this end. Some of you have been in the business world for years, but this is still a decision you must face: will you serve the Lord or will you make the business world the dominating thing in your life? The most subtle temptations come to a man through his success in the business world. God multiplies his business, increases the material remunerations from that business, and first thing you know, that man because of his success has become so wedded to his business that the things of God fade and grow dim. He started out on a hand-to-mouth existence with a determination to serve God, and when God blessed, that determination somehow was lost, and he finds out that business has taken control. He is serving it and has lost sight of the fact that he cannot serve God and mammon.

I realize that I am in as privileged a position as a man could be in, and I thank God for it every day. I realize that businessmen have problems that I don't have. Day after day it is my privilege to handle the Word of God, teaching and preaching. My contacts are almost entirely with people who are preparing for the ministry or with those who have come to know Jesus Christ as Saviour and want to be taught the Word of God. That is an enviable position for any man to be in. God has laid it upon my heart to pray much for those who have to mingle day after day in a hostile world. Because as a pastor I have talked with so many businessmen, I understand somewhat the problems they face, and this is the central issue in any businessman's life: Will I serve God or mammon? If you are going to set God in the preeminent place, you must be prepared to pay the price that the business world asks of those who set Jesus Christ before everything else. You may have to reevaluate your goals, standards, methods, and measurements of success; but what can be higher than to have God's approval and to have the assurance that we have been faithful to the stewardship entrusted to

us? You who may be facing the business world from day to
day, which will it be? God or business? The decision has to
be yours.

15

God's Answer to

THE PROBLEM OF MATERIALISM

MATTHEW 6:19-34

The problem of the relation of a man to material things seems to be a problem as old as man himself, for the writers of Scripture are constantly dealing with man's attitude toward material possessions. That which seems to be particularly a present-day problem is a problem dealt with in many different instances in the Word of God. We must recognize that we are living in the richest, most affluent society that the world has known, but there have been other affluent societies.

Israel was an affluent society, and their affluence was a sign of God's blessing upon them. God did not condemn them because of what they possessed, but rather, because of their attitude toward what they had. When God chose the nation Israel He promised that nation peculiar blessings if they would walk in the path of obedience, and the blessings He promised were material. When the Israelites were about to enter the promised land, Moses reiterated God's promise that He would heap material blessings upon them if they obeyed His Word in the new land (Deu 28). The blessings that God gave them were not what we would refer to as spiritual blessings at all, but they were blessings of flocks, herds, and material possessions. And conversely, God also warned them that if they walked in disobedience He would take away all their material blessings and shut up the windows of heaven; there would be no rain and there would be no harvest. Through the Old Testament a sign of God's displeasure was a famine; but the sure sign of God's approval was a bountiful harvest.

God did not speak in any disapproving way of material possessions nor disapprove of those who acquired material wealth; but He did deal constantly with the problem of the individual's attitude toward that wealth. Israel as an affluent society in the midst of surrounding nations was hated because they were a blessed and a wealthy people, but God did not say they should not have their goods because they were despised and hated. They were to use them as unto the Lord. However, Israel developed a perverted attitude toward material things and, by the time the New Testament era arrived, they had developed a philosophy about material things: "Whom the Lord loveth, He maketh rich." In a measure this was true, but it was only a partial truth, and they began to view material possession as the chief end of man. Thus, when Christ taught about this important subject, He still did not condemn material possessions nor the acquisition of material possessions; but He did condemn trusting in material possessions, and making them the end and goal of life. The words He spoke and what the apostles later wrote concerning material things are certainly what we need to heed today; because, in comparison with those of His day, there is not one of us who would not be considered an outstandingly wealthy man.

The Word of God does distinguish between material things and spiritual things (see Mt 6). Material things are things of this earth—things that appeal to the senses. Spiritual things are the things that belong to heaven and cannot be grasped, discovered, nor appropriated by the physical senses. The Lord made it very clear that there are earthly treasures as well as heavenly treasures, and the earthly treasures are material and the heavenly treasures are spiritual. That which is material has value only because man attributes value to it. It is not valuable because of what it is in itself, but because of the value that man places upon it. After all, there is practically no difference between a diamond and a lump of coal. You put value on one and no value on the other. One ends up in the jewelry shop; the other is cast into the furnace. There is little difference between gold and iron, but one is highly esteemed and the other despised. It is man's attitude toward those things that gives them value.

Not so with spiritual things. Spiritual things have value because of the value that God places upon them as opposed to the value that man places upon material things. Material things of necessity cater to the flesh. Spiritual things can appeal only to the new man in Christ Jesus. The man who has never been born again has to have something to which he gives himself, and all that he can pursue is something material. But the man who has been born again has an entirely new set of values and can give himself to the pursuit of spiritual things. The apostle Paul makes this clear in telling Timothy that the greatest gain is godliness with contentment (1 Ti 6:6). Notice that he is contrasting that which has spiritual value—godliness with contentment—with material things; and Paul makes several well-known statements: "For we brought nothing into this world, and it is certain we can carry nothing out" (6:7). He is pointing out that material things are earthly. They are temporary and transitory. They are related to time and not to eternity, for we came into the world with nothing and we will go out of the world and leave all material things behind.

"And having food and raiment let us be therewith content. But they that will be rich fall into temptation and a snare, and into many foolish and hurtful lusts" (6:8-9). Notice that the apostle did not say they that *are* rich, because a rich man can know godliness with contentment, but he said those who *will* be rich. He is emphasizing the attitude toward those material things of the individual who does not have them. They have become the aim, goal and the master in life. The person who lusts after material things, finds that his lust controls him. He seeks to acquire those things by any means possible, right or wrong. Because of this Paul says that "the love of money is the root of all evil" (v. 10). Money is not the root of all evil, but the *love* of money, by the one who does not have it, is the root of all evil. The man who has material things may love them, but the man who doesn't have them probably loves them more. The man who has things realizes how unlovely they actually are. But the person who doesn't have them has convinced himself that they are lovable, and he lusts after them. So when Paul was talking to believers who wanted to become rich, he warned that the love of money was the root of all evil. Paul warned Timothy, ". . . which while some coveted after, they have erred from the faith, and pierced themselves through with many sorrows. But thou, O man of God, flee these things" (vv. 10*b*-11*a*).

If in his ministry he pursued money, then he would be led away from the faith. He would have a false love, a false affection, a false goal in his ministry, and would be led into foolish and hurtful lusts. Paul was saying that the love of money appeals to the flesh and that the fleshly man gives himself to these material things. The term *money* refers to all material possessions, whether it be the actual coin on deposit in the bank or whether it be the material things that can be acquired with money: houses, furnishings, cars, and all the rest of the things for which money may be used.

Paul's great emphasis in this passage is on the fact that material things cater to the flesh and that pride of possession or acquisition, or a pride in the power that the possessions bring, will become a snare and trap to a man. In Matthew 6:19-20, the Lord mentions that material things are temporary. They are concerned with this physical life here and now. He contrasts the earthly treasure with the heavenly treasure. The earthly treasure decays or it may be plundered by a thief. Contrariwise, that which is not material, the true spiritual treasure, is not temporary. It is not corruptible and cannot be stolen by any thief. We are creatures in time, and we cannot think in terms of eternity. God is the eternal one and does not think in terms of time. We put our whole emphasis on what is here and now, what is of the earth—that which can be touched, handled, measured and weighed. Not so God. Giving the divine viewpoint, Christ says these material things are temporary.

How foolish it is to focus attention and love upon that which is bound to pass away. The great tragedy is that we are giving our effort and affection toward that which must pass away because it is corruptible. All that comes from the earth is under the curse. Looking at diamonds, gold or silver, we somehow feel that they have been exempted from the curse on this earth. But they are just as cursed as any other part of creation because of the fall of man. Because creation is cursed, it must be judged. After the millennial kingdom of our Lord, Peter tells us, this earth will be judged by fire. The elements within the earth shall be consumed by what appears to be one mighty atomic disintegration and all that is material and under the curse will be no more. That will include the diamonds, rubies, silver and the gold as well as the thorns on this earth. So that which is material is temporary; it is corruptible; it is under judgment. If a child of God loves and lusts after material things, he is loving and seeking that which is under the God's curse and will be destroyed.

The second thing Christ said concerning these material things was that they can enslave a man. "No man can serve two masters: for either he will hate the one, and love the other; or else he will hold to the one, and despise the other. Ye cannot serve God and mammon" (Mt 6:24). The word "mammon" refers to all material things. Notice that He did not say, "A man *usually* does not serve God and mammon." He stated it as an utter impossibility. "Ye *cannot* serve God and mammon." No man can be faithful to two masters. If he is faithful to the master of mammon, he will be faithless to God; and if he is faithful to God, he cannot give himself to the pursuit of material things with divine blessing. It is an either-or proposition. The reason is, "Where your treasure is, there will your heart be also" (v. 21). What a man loves he will pursue, and if a man loves material things he will pursue material things; if he loves God, he will pursue God. The psalmist David, one of the richest men of his day, passed through the experience of having material things and finding that they couldn't satisfy him. He said, "As the hart panteth after the water brooks, so panteth my soul after thee, O God" (Ps 42:1). His heart was given over to the pursuit of God. If a man gives himself over to the pursuit of material things for what they are in themselves, then he will be faithless as a servant of God.

The third thing Christ points out in this passage is that the pursuit of material things is a false, empty and vain goal in life (vv. 25-33). He says this is what characterized the Gentiles: "After all these things did the Gentiles seek" (Mt 6:32). Paul said that Gentiles had a vain or an empty mind (Eph 4:17-18). They could not be characterized as spiritual; there was nothing spiritual about them. That which characterized them was their love of material things. In visiting the ruins of the ancient societies of the day in which Paul lived, it is quite evident that the people loved material things. They built beautiful buildings, the ruins of which remain today in Athens, Rome and other cities. They paved their floors with fine mosaics, and had beautiful gardens. Things that fill our museums today bear testimony to the fact that the Gentiles were given over to pursuit of these material things. In pursuing them they loved and served them, and material things became the sum total of life for the Greeks and the Romans.

Christ told the believers, "Don't fall into the pattern of thinking of the empty-headed Gentiles. You seek first the kingdom of God and His righteousness." That is a true spiritual goal. And then our Lord adds the promise that God will provide the man who pursues Him with all the material things he needs: "Seek ye first the kingdom of God, and his righteousness; and all these things shall be added unto you (Mt. 6:33). A man will not put the kingdom of God first unless he loves God with all his heart and soul and mind. If he is of a divided mind, he cannot seek God's kingdom first. So Christ said that if they, like Gentiles, pursued material things, they would find themselves in constant need. But if they would seek first the kingdom of God and His righteousness, and that would become their goal, a faithful Father would provide all that they needed. On that basis Paul could write, "My God shall supply all your needs according to his riches in glory by Christ Jesus" (Phil 4:19). It is a vain goal to strive for and lust after that which is temporary and transitory, but the true goal is to pursue the kingdom of God and His righteousness and then all of these material things shall be supplied.

In 1 Peter 5, Peter addresses a word to the elders, those who were ministering to the flock of God and had responsibilities to the flock. He tells them, "Feed the flock of God which is among you, taking the oversight thereof, not by constraint, but willingly." Now notice these words: "Not for filthy lucre, but of a ready mind" (v. 2). Paul's principle laid down in the epistle to the Corinthians was that those who preached the gospel should live of the gospel. When it was necessary because there were no believers, Paul worked with his hands making tents. But as soon as a nucleus of believers existed, Paul expected to have his material needs met by those believers on the basis of that principle. But this involved a temptation. Some might say that they would rather be an elder or pastor than to work. Thus Peter counseled them that when they were given the opportunity of feeding the flock of God, it was not to be for filthy lucre. He was pointing out that the pursuit of material things may provide a false motive in service. Christ spoke about a false goal, but now Peter is talking about a false motive, accepting a responsibility purely for the monetary reward involved in discharging that responsibility. If one accepts God's will with a view to the material remuneration, then he is operating on the basis of a false motive. The first question a man asks when he is considering a change in his position is, What is the salary? The graduate getting out of college wants to know what the present salary is and how much the pension will be. That becomes his motive in life, and the Lord is left out of the consideration. He does not consider the spiritual: What is God's will? But rather, he thinks of how the material: How much will I be paid? So Peter warns about accepting material things as the motive in life.

Another writer who deals extensively with this problem of material things is James. He addresses a word to the rich who were the persecutors of the poor (5:1-6). His teaching can be summarized by saying that the pursuit of material things does not bring happiness. "Go to now, ye rich men, weep and howl for your miseries that shall come upon you" (v. 1). A rich man miserable? Yes. James begins by pointing out that these rich men were miserable. They weren't miserable because they had money; it was because they loved the money. It had become their motive and goal and the end in life, and money couldn't satisfy them; therefore misery came upon them because they were not seeking first the kingdom of God and His righteousness.

"Your riches are corrupted, and your garments are moth-eaten. Your gold and silver is cankered; and the rust of them shall be a witness against you" (vv. 2-3a). James, like our Lord, is emphasizing the temporary and transitory character of these riches. "Ye have heaped treasure together for the last days" (v. 3b). These rich had fallen into sin for they were getting rich by robbing the poor. "The hire of the labourers who have reaped down your fields, which is of you kept back by fraud, crieth. . . . Ye have lived in pleasure on the earth, and been wanton; ye have nourished your hearts, as in a day of slaughter. Ye have condemned and killed the just; and he doth not resist you" (vv. 4-6). Thus James shows that the pursuit of material things does not bring happiness, but promotes sin. Man was created as a spiritual being when God breathed into his nostrils the breath of life, and a spiritual being cannot be satisfied with material things. An ox was created to be nourished by grass, but a lion was not; and you could dump bales of hay into the lions' den and it would never nourish the lion. Or you could throw meat to the ox and the ox could never be nourished by it. Man is a spiritual being and, even though he is spiritually dead, he still cannot be truly satisfied by material things. James says that those who pursue and love these materal things will be miserable because things cannot bring happiness. God is the only one who can satisfy the longing of the human heart.

Peter taught in 1 Peter 1:18-19 that material things cannot provide salvation for a sinner. "Forasmuch as you know that we were not redeemed with corruptible things" (v. 18). Material things are temporary, transitory, and under the curse and, because they are accursed, they cannot remove sin. They cannot provide redemption, but you were "redeemed . . . with the precious blood of Christ, as of a lamb without blemish and without spot" (vv. 18-19). The child of God is faced with a choice by which he must determine the course of his life. Will it be material or spiritual things? Will it be love of money or will it be love of God? Perhaps the classic example of one who made that choice is in Hebrews 11:

> By faith Moses, when he was born, was hid three months of his parents, because they saw he was a proper child; and they were not afraid of the king's commandment. By faith Moses, when he was come to years, refused to be called the son of Pharaoh's daughter; choosing rather to suffer affliction with the people of God, than to enjoy the pleasures of sin for a season; esteeming the reproach of Christ greater riches than the treasures in Egypt (vv. 23-26).

Egypt was one of the richest nations that ever existed upon the face of the earth. A visit to the Cairo Museum will convince anyone that Egypt had boundless wealth. King Tut was one of the insignificant kings of Egypt, who died when he was perhaps twenty-one. His body was encased in a gold coffin that is valued at more than fifteen million dollars. Egypt was rich, and Moses, because of his adoption into the royal family, was heir to its riches.

So Moses was confronted with a choice. It was the choice of the pursuit of these material things or a life of privation and separation to God. He chose to suffer affliction with the people of God rather than enjoy the pleasures of sin for a season, considering the reproach that he bore for Christ's sake greater riches than the treasures of Egypt. And Moses made a decisive choice; he chose God and turned his back on man. But even though Moses rejected Egypt's treasures, he never went hungry a day in his life. God had to perform a miracle of bringing manna from heaven, but He saw to it that the one who made that choice was fed. Moses never went thirsty. Even though God had to open a rock and bring water out of it, He saw to it that Moses never went thirsty. Moses never lacked shoes even during years of wilderness experiences because God accepted the responsibility of providing for him.

While the Word of God nowhere condemns the possession of material things, it does condemn the love of material things. There is often a very fine dividing line between the two. How can you test whether you're rightly related to your material possessions? Ask these questions: What is it that dominates and controls my life? Am I a slave to these things? Is the possession of them my goal? And if you have to answer in the affirmative, then you are transgressing Christ's commandment to lay not up for yourselves treasures on earth. But if you can look at those things and realize that they are what the Word says they are—transitory, material, and part of the curse—and then forsake them, if that is your attitude toward them, then you can have them with God's approval. But one's attitude is often difficult to discern. Good questions to ask are, Could I get along without it? If all these things were stripped away, would I consider myself a pauper? Or are these simply some of the little embellishments that make life enjoyable that I could get along without if I had to? If one is seeking the kingdom of God first, these things can come or go. If one is pursuing these things, they can't go without a man feeling a sense of loss and considering himself a pauper, bereft of all his treasures.

It comes down to this: What are our riches? Where is our wealth deposited? Is it in Christ, or is it in these material things? Paul said that God gives us all things richly to enjoy. This certainly includes our material possessions. Here faith fails and we are ashamed to enjoy things that God has given us. We have felt it is wrong to have possessions. But Paul said God has given us all things richly to enjoy. It is true that any blessing that God has given to man may be perverted by man. God has given us food to enjoy. But there is a difference between being a gourmet and a glutton; and when we become gluttonous, we do not have the proper attitude toward food. Things may be used or they may be perverted and misused. We must guard against corrupting that which God has given. In these things that were given for us to enjoy, may we be brought in such subjection to the Lord Jesus Christ that it will be evident to all that we are seeking first Christ and His righteousness, that He is preeminent in life, and that all falls into insignificance alongside Him. Use these material things to gain permanent treasures. Make them means unto an end and not the end in itself.